ARTIFICIAL INTELLIGENCE FOR PHARMACEUTICAL AUDIT SURVIVAL

HOW REGULATED AI IS REDEFINING AUDIT READINESS

AMIT KUMAR GURU

notionpress.com

INDIA • SINGAPORE • MALAYSIA

ISBN
Paperback 979-8-90342-259-3
Hardcase 979-8-90431-656-3

Disclaimer

This ebook is intended for **educational and informational purposes only**.

It does not constitute legal advice, regulatory advice, or professional consulting services.

While every effort has been made to ensure accuracy and alignment with current pharmaceutical regulatory principles, standards, and guidelines (including but not limited to ICH, FDA, EMA, WHO, and other global agencies), regulations and interpretations may change over time. The author makes no guarantees regarding completeness, accuracy, or applicability to specific regulatory situations.

Readers are advised to consult appropriate regulatory authorities, qualified professionals, or official guidance documents before making decisions related to compliance, audits, or quality systems.

No Regulatory Endorsement

This publication is an independent work.

References to regulatory agencies, standards, or guidance documents are made for explanatory purposes only and do not imply endorsement, approval, or affiliation by any regulatory authority.

No Software or Tool Promotion

Any references to artificial intelligence, automation, or analytical approaches are conceptual and illustrative in nature.

This book does not promote, endorse, or require the use of any specific software, vendor, platform, or technology solution.

Limitation of Liability

The author shall not be liable for any direct, indirect, incidental, consequential, or commercial damages arising from the use, interpretation, or application of information contained in this publication.

Use of the material in this ebook is entirely at the reader's own discretion and risk.

Intellectual Property Notice

All trademarks, service marks, product names, and company names mentioned in this book are the property of their respective owners and are used for identification purposes only.

Contents

About the Author *xxvii*

Acknowledgement *xxxi*

When Compliance Became Too Complex for Spreadsheets *xxxvii*

The Industry's Unspoken Transition *xxxvii*

A Question Every Inspector Already Asks *xxxviii*

Why This Moment Is Different *xxxviii*

What This Book Refuses to Do *xxxix*

What This Book Is Really About *xxxix*

Why Chapter One Starts Now *xl*

Chapter 1: The Audit Fear Nobody Talks About **1**

The Quietest Room in the Plant 1

1. Anatomy of an Unspoken Fear 2

2. From Fear to Audit Failure: The Causal Chain 3

3. Traditional Coping Mechanisms—and Why They Fall Short 4

4. Where AI-Assisted Visibility Changes the Game 5

5. Common Mistakes When Reaching for Technology 6

6. The "Continuous Transparency" Framework 7

7. Field Story: The Calibration Catastrophe That Never Happened 8

8. Mistake Autopsies: Learning from Pain 9

9. Practical Mindset Shift: From Gatekeeping to Storytelling 10

10. Key Takeaways 11

Chapter 2: We Were Compliant… On Paper 12

A Curious Compliment 12

1. The Illusion of "Binder Compliance" 12

2. Where the Mirage Comes From 13

3. How the Mirage Trips Audits 14

4. Case Study: The Cleanroom That Failed in the Database 15

5. Why Traditional Fixes Fail 15

6. Where AI and Automation Help—Without the Hype 16

7. Common Missteps When Digitizing Compliance 17

8. The Living Compliance Pyramid: A Framework 18

9. Mindset Shift: From Narrative to Evidence 19

10. Key Takeaways 19

Looking Ahead 20

Chapter 3: How Inspectors Actually Think 21

Welcome Back—From Paper Reality to the Inspector's Reality 21

1. The Inspector's Mandate: Public Health, Not Paperwork 21

2. Risk-Based Triaging: How Limited Time Shapes Their Focus 22

3. The "Smell Test": First Five Minutes, Lasting Impressions 23

4. Building the Story: Inspectors as Investigative Journalists 23

5. Cognitive Toolkit: Pattern Recognition, Triangulation, and Outlier Hunting 24

6. Why Traditional "Inspection Readiness" Often Fails 25

7. Inside the Interview Room: Verbal and Non-Verbal Signals 25

8. Escalation Pathways: From Curiosity to Concern to Compliance Action 26

9. Case Study: The Spectrophotometer That Sank a Site 26

10. Where AI and Automation Enter the Picture—But Only Later 27

11. Common Missteps to Avoid When "Reading" Inspectors 28

12. A Practical Framework: The Credibility Loop 28

13. Putting It All Together 29

14. Key Takeaways 30

Transition to Part 2 30

Chapter 4: Why Manual Compliance Is Breaking Pharma **31**

A Quick Look Back—and a Glimpse Ahead 31

1. The Legacy of Manual Compliance 31
2. The Hidden Physics of Human Error 32
3. Compliance Debt: The Quiet Accumulation of Risk 33
4. Audit-Time Shock: When Manual Systems Freeze 34
5. A Case Study: The Day the Temperature Logs Betrayed Us 35
6. Traditional Fixes—and Why They Fail 35
7. Where AI and Automation Can Help—But Only If Framed Correctly 36
8. Common Pitfalls When Shifting from Manual to Automated Compliance 37
9. A Practical Framework: The Human-Machine Risk Lens 38
10. Key Takeaways 39

Wrapping Up—and Setting the Stage 39

Chapter 5: AI Is Not Magic (And That's Why It Works) **41**

A Quick Breath Before We Dive In 41

1. Why "Magic" Thinking Creeps Into Pharma in the First Place 42
2. How "Magic" Thinking Leads Straight to Audit Findings 42

3. Why Traditional Corrective Actions Fall Short 43
4. De-Mystifying AI: How It Really Works in Plain Language 44
5. Where AI Genuinely Excels—and Why That Matters in an Audit 45
6. Guardrails: A Practical Framework I Use With Clients 46
7. Common Pitfalls I Keep Seeing 47
8. A Day in the Life: How Realistic AI Fits a QA Professional's Routine 47
9. From Inspector Questions to Framework Answers 48
10. The Mindset Shift You and I Must Embrace 49
11. Key Takeaways From This Chapter 49
12. Transitioning to the Next Chapter 50

Chapter 6: Automation vs Over-Automation 51

A Brief Look Back 51
1. Why the Temptation to Automate Everything Exists 51
2. How Over-Automation Breeds New Audit Failures 53
3. Traditional Mitigation Strategies—and Their Limits 54
4. Where AI and Automation Genuinely Help—If You Apply Restraint 55
5. Common Mistakes When Pursuing "Lights-Out" Quality 57

6. A Practical Framework: The Automation Balance Canvas 58

7. Illustrative Scenario: Filling Line Out-of-Spec Alerts 59

8. The Human Dimension: Teaching "Judicious Laziness" 61

9. Regulatory Perspectives on Automation Scope 62

10. Key Takeaways 62

Transition to Part 3 63

Chapter 7: AI-Powered Audit Readiness (Daily, Not Event-Based) 64

Setting the Scene—Why "Audit Readiness" Is Usually an Illusion 64

1. Why the Fire-Drill Model of Audit Preparation Persists 65

2. How Event-Based Readiness Fails During Real Audits 65

3. The Continuous Readiness Philosophy 66

4. Where Traditional Approaches Fall Short 67

5. What "AI-Powered" Really Means in Daily Practice 68

6. Core Capabilities of AI-Powered Readiness 68

7. Daily Workflow—A Walk-Through Example 70

8. Architecting the System Without Over-Engineering 71

9. Governance and Human Oversight 71

10. Common Mistakes to Avoid 72

11. A Practical Framework—The Five-Layer Model of Daily AI Readiness 73

12. Cultivating the Right Mindset 73

13. Case Study—Turning a Crisis Into Continuous Readiness 74

14. Key Takeaways 75

Transition to Next Chapter 75

Chapter 8: Preventing Data Integrity Failures Before They Happen 76

A Natural Next Step 76

1. Why Data Integrity Keeps Slipping Through the Cracks 77

2. How Data Integrity Failures Trigger Audit Disasters 78

3. Why Classical Controls Stall 79

4. Where AI and Automation Provide Real, Regulator-Friendly Help 79

5. Common Pitfalls When Introducing AI-Driven Monitoring 81

6. A Pragmatic Framework: The ADEPT Model 81

7. Implementation Roadmap Without Vendor Hype 82

8. Case Study—Catching the Invisible Injection Peak 84

9. Human Factors Still Matter—Bridging Technology and Culture 85

10. Regulatory Alignment Check 85

11. Key Takeaways 86

A Glance Forward 86

Chapter 9: Smart Document Review & Reducing Human Blind Spots **87**

Lead-In from the Previous Chapter 87

1. Why the Document Problem Exists 87
2. How Blind Spots Cause Audit Failures 88
3. Why Traditional Approaches Fall Short 89
4. Where AI-Driven Review Genuinely Helps 90
5. A Practical Framework: The Five-Level Smart Review Loop 91
6. Case Study: The Discreet Torque Mismatch 92
7. Regulatory Alignment: Showing Inspectors the Logic 92
8. Common Mistakes to Avoid 93
9. Implementation Playbook 93
10. Metrics That Matter 94
11. From "Approve and File" to "Question and Correlate"—The Mindset Shift 95
12. Key Takeaways 95

Smooth Transition to the Next Chapter 96

Chapter 10: Smart Document Review & Reducing Human Blind Spots **97**

A Lead-In From Data Integrity 97

1. Why Documentation Trips Up Even the Best Teams 97
2. Anatomy of an "Almost Perfect" SOP 99

3. Traditional Document Control: Where It Helps and Where It Hinders 100

4. Enter AI-Assisted Document Review (But Not Replacement) 100

5. Four Core Capabilities You Need 101

6. Realistic Scenario: The Misaligned Batch Record 102

7. Common Mistakes to Avoid When Automating Document Review 103

8. Building a Human + AI Review Workflow 104

9. Metrics That Actually Matter 105

10. The Mindset Shift: From Archiving to Living Documents 105

11. Key Takeaways 106

Chapter 11: How Careers Get Damaged During Audits 107

A Quiet Corridor After the Audit—And the Whisper You Never Forget 107

1. Why Audit Findings Become Personal Even When They Sound Procedural 108

2. Mechanisms of Career Damage During and After Audits 109

3. Why Traditional Audit-Preparation Approaches Fail to Protect Individuals 110

4. Where AI and Intelligent Automation Provide Personal Career Protection 111

5. Common Missteps When Implementing AI for Individual Protection 112

6. A Practical Framework: The Personal Risk Heat-Map 113

7. A True Story—Names Changed, Lessons Preserved 114

8. Mindset Shift: From Defensive Posture to Proactive Transparency 115

9. Key Takeaways 116

10. Looking Ahead—From Personal Survival to Collective Resilience 116

Chapter 12: AI for Deviations, CAPAs & Change Controls 117

The Quiet Pivot From Static Documents to Living Quality Events 117

1. Why Deviations, CAPAs, and Change Controls Are Audit Landmines 118

2. How the Problem Blossoms Into Audit Findings 119

3. Traditional Approaches and Their Shortfalls 119

4. Where AI Genuinely Adds Value 121

5. A Case Study—From Firefighting to Forecasting 123

6. Common Missteps to Avoid 124

7. A Practical Framework—The R.A.I.S.E. Model 125

8. Ethical and Regulatory Guardrails 126

9. Transitioning to the Next Frontier 127

10. Key Takeaways 128

Chapter 13: Making AI Regulator-Friendly **129**

A Quick Look Back—and a Hard Look Forward 129

1. Why "Regulator-Friendly" Even Matters 129
2. How "Unfriendly" AI Triggers Audit Failures 130
3. Why Traditional Approaches Fall Short 131
4. Where AI Actually Helps the Regulator—If You Let It 131
5. The Six Principles of Regulator-Friendly AI 132
6. A Day in the Life—A Practical Walk-Through 134
7. Common Mistakes to Avoid 135
8. The AI–GxP Alignment Canvas 136
9. A Note on Global Regulatory Nuances 137
10. Building Trust—One Dialogue at a Time 137
11. Mindset Shift: From Proof to Story 137
12. Key Takeaways 138

Seamless Transition to the Next Chapter 138

Chapter 14: Training People to Think, Not Just Click **139**

A Quick Look Back—From Regulator-Friendly Technology to Regulator-Ready People 139

1. Why "Click Training" Became the Default 139
2. Consequences in the Audit Room 140
3. Why Traditional Approaches Fail Under AI Pressure 141

4. The Cognitive Gap: Soft Skills Meet System Skills 142

5. Principles of Effective AI-Era Training 142

6. The Four Levels of Audit-Conscious Thinking 143

7. Embedding AI Literacy Without Turning Everyone into Data Scientists 144

8. The DECIDE Framework—A Practical Cognitive Workflow 144

9. A Day in the Life—QC Analyst with an AI Assistant 145

10. Cross-Functional Mock Audits Using AI Simulations 146

11. Building a Culture of Challenge and Curiosity 146

12. Common Pitfalls to Avoid 147

13. Measuring Training Effectiveness—Leading vs Lagging Indicators 147

14. Regulatory Expectations on Training Records in the AI Era 148

15. Case Study—Biologics Plant that Rewired Its Training Approach 148

16. Key Takeaways 149

Bridging to the Next Chapter 149

Chapter 15: Training People to Think, Not Just Click 151

A Brief Look Back—and Forward 151

1. Why "Click Training" Took Over Pharma 151

2. The Unseen Risk: Procedural Compliance Without Cognitive Engagement 152

3. Cognitive Compliance: What Inspectors Look For 153

4. Skill Sets for the AI-Enabled Quality Professional 154

5. Designing Training That Builds Judgment 155

6. Embedding Critical Thinking Into Daily GxP Tasks 156

7. Simulation-Based Learning: A Practical Blueprint 157

8. Metrics That Matter: Measuring Thinking, Not Just Completion 158

9. Overcoming Resistance: From Fear of Automation to Ownership 159

10. Sustaining a Learning Culture in a High-Pressure Environment 160

11. Common Pitfalls to Avoid 160

12. Mindset Framework: Observe—Question—Explain—Decide (OQED) 161

13. Key Takeaways 162

Chapter 16: Training People to Think, Not Just Click 164

A Quick Look Back 164

1. The Illusion of "System-Trained" Personnel 164

2. Clicking Through SOPs: The Uncomfortable Reality 165

3. The Cognitive Gap Inspectors Spot in Minutes 166

4. Why Traditional Training Programs Stagnate 166

5. Thinking Frameworks vs. Button Paths 167

6. Where AI Becomes a Silent Coach 168

7. Designing a Risk-Literate Workforce 168

8. Continual Learning Loops: From Shift Log to Neural Net 169

9. Mistakes to Avoid When Rolling Out AI-Enabled Training 169

10. The "Ask Why Twice" Model—A Practical Framework 170

11. Case Study: A Batch Record Near-Miss Averted 171

12. From Compliance Anxiety to Situational Awareness 172

13. Key Takeaways 172

Transition to Next Chapter 173

Chapter 17: The Future of Audits Will Be Boring (And That's Good) 174

A Natural Lead-In 174

1. Why "Boring" Is the Ultimate KPI 174

2. From Firefighting to Flow 175

3. The Emerging Regulatory Landscape 175

4. AI as Invisible Infrastructure 176

5. A Day in 2030: What an Audit Looks Like 177

6. Evolving Roles: From Documentation Clerks to Risk Strategists 178

7. New Metrics: Signal-to-Noise Ratio Over Paper Volume 179

8. Ethical Guardrails in a Hyper-Automated World 179

9. Common Illusions About the Future—And How to Avoid Them 180

10. Building Your Personal Roadmap Toward the Boring Audit 181

11. Closing Thoughts: A Final Conversation Between Future You and Today You 181

12. Key Takeaways 182

Chapter 18: Artificial Intelligence as an Enabler of Pharmaceutical Quality: Aligning Innovation with ICH Q10 and ICH Q11 183

Introduction: AI Does Not Replace the Quality System—It Reveals It 183

1. Understanding the Intent of ICH Q10 Before Introducing AI 184

2. AI and Knowledge Management: The Missing Link in ICH Q10 Execution 185

3. Process Performance and Product Quality Monitoring: From Reactive to Predictive 185

4. AI and CAPA Systems: Strengthening Root Cause Analysis, Not Replacing It 186

5. Change Management Under ICH Q10: AI as an Impact Visibility Tool 187

6. Management Review: Turning Data into Meaningful Oversight 188

7. ICH Q11: Scientific Understanding as the Foundation of AI Use 188

8. AI and Control Strategy Optimization Under ICH Q11 189

9. Lifecycle Management: Where ICH Q10 and Q11 Truly Meet AI 189

10. Regulatory Acceptability: The Conditions Under Which AI Aligns with ICH 190

11. The Human Role Remains Central 190

12. Conclusion: AI as a Maturity Test of the Quality System 191

Chapter 19: Artificial Intelligence and Quality Risk Management During Pharmaceutical Audits 192

1. Introduction: Why Risk Management, Not AI, Decides Audit Outcomes 192
2. The Regulator's View of Quality Risk Management During Audits 193
3. The Structural Weaknesses of Traditional QRM in Pharma 194
4. Fragmented Risk Ownership 194
5. Retrospective Risk Recognition 194
6. Inconsistent Risk Scoring 195
7. Artificial Intelligence as a Risk Visibility Layer 195
8. Quality Risk Management Across Audit Phases 196
9. Pre-Audit Phase: Risk Anticipation 196
10. During the Audit: Risk Exposure Management 196

11. Post-Audit Phase: Risk-Based CAPA and Remediation 197
12. AI and Risk Identification: Seeing What Humans Miss 197
13. Risk Analysis and Evaluation: Supporting, Not Automating Decisions 198
14. Risk Control: Making Controls Proportionate and Effective 198
15. Risk Communication and Documentation: Audit Transparency 199
16. Governance of AI Within QRM 199
17. Interim Reflection: AI Does Not Reduce Risk—It Reduces Blindness 199
18. Re-anchoring AI Within the Principles of ICH Q9 200
19. AI and Risk Identification Under ICH Q9: Moving Beyond Obvious Risks 201
20. The Human Limitation in Risk Identification 201
21. AI's Contribution: Weak Signal Detection 201
22. Risk Analysis: Where Most QRM Systems Collapse Under Audit Pressure 202
23. Audit Observations Related to Weak Risk Analysis 202
24. How AI Supports Risk Analysis Without Violating Regulatory Expectations 202
25. Risk Evaluation: Prioritization Under Scrutiny 203
26. Why Prioritization Fails During Audits 203
27. AI as a Risk Prioritization Consistency Tool 203
28. AI and Risk Control: Aligning Controls With Actual Risk 204

29. Over-Control as an Audit Liability 204
30. AI's Role in Control Effectiveness Assessment 205
31. Risk Review and Lifecycle Monitoring: The Audit Time Bomb 205
32.Audit Failures Linked to Static Risk Assessments 205
33. AI as a Continuous Risk Review Mechanism 205
34. Quality Risk Management During Live Audits: What Inspectors Actually Test 206
35. AI and Data Integrity Risk Management During Audits 206
36. Why Data Integrity Risks Evade Traditional QRM 207
37. AI as an Early Warning System for Data Integrity 207
38. Boundaries: What AI Must Never Do in QRM 207
39. Cultural Impact: AI as a Risk Maturity Indicator 208
40. Interim Conclusion: Risk Visibility Is the Real Regulatory Advantage 208
41. Why Auditors Don't Fear Data—They Fear Blind Spots 208
42. Static Risk Management vs Living Risk Management 209
43. Traditional QRM (Audit Reality) 209
44. AI-Enabled Living Risk Management 210
45. Risk Identification: From Human Memory to System Awareness 210
46. Audit Challenge 210
47. AI's Role in Risk Identification 211
48. Risk Analysis: Moving Beyond Subjective Scoring 211

49. The Problem with Traditional Risk Scoring 211

50. How AI Strengthens Risk Analysis 212

51. Risk Control: Monitoring Effectiveness, Not Just Implementation 212

52. Audit Reality 212

53. AI in Risk Control Monitoring 213

54. Risk Communication: Speaking the Auditor's Language 213

55. Common Audit Failure 213

56. AI-Supported Risk Communication 214

57. Risk Review: The Most Overlooked QRM Element 214

58. AI as a Risk Review Trigger 215

59. What Auditors Actually See When AI Supports QRM 215

60. AI Does Not Reduce Accountability—It Increases It 216

61. Transitioning from Risk Documentation to Risk Stewardship 216

62.The Silent Shift in How Audits Are Conducted 217

63. How Inspectors Prioritize Risk During Audits 218

64. Risk-Based Sampling and AI Readiness 218

65. Inspector Confidence vs Organizational Confidence 219

66. Over-Automation Without Governance 220

67. Black-Box Risk Decisions 220

68. Using AI Without Updating SOPs 220

69. Treating AI Outputs as "Truth" 221

70. Fragmented AI Usage Across Departments 221

71. Start with QRM Principles—Not Technology 221
72. Clear Role Definition 222
73. Data Integrity as a Prerequisite 222
74. Governance and Oversight 222
75. Training the Human System 222
76. Audits Are Personal—Whether We Admit It or Not 223
77. From Firefighter to Risk Leader 223
78. Accountability Without Anxiety 224
79. Final Reflection for Chapter 19 224

Chapter 20: Artificial Intelligence and CAPA Remediation During Pharmaceutical Audits 225

1. CAPA: The True Measure of a Quality System 225
2. Why CAPA Fails in Otherwise "Compliant" Organizations 226
3. CAPA in the Auditor's Mindset 226
4. The Structural Weakness of Traditional CAPA Systems 227
5. Where Artificial Intelligence Fits—and Where It Does Not 228
6. AI and CAPA Triggering: Detecting Issues Earlier 228
7. AI-Supported Root Cause Analysis (RCA) 229
8. CAPA Design: From Action Lists to System Corrections 229
9. Preventive Action: The Most Misunderstood CAPA Element 230
10. CAPA Effectiveness: The Audit's Deciding Factor 230

11. CAPA During Live Audits: What Changes with AI 231
12. CAPA Traceability and Knowledge Retention 232
13. AI, CAPA, and Management Review 232
14. Data Integrity and AI-Supported CAPA 233
15. Validation and Governance Expectations 233
16. Common AI–CAPA Mistakes That Trigger Observations 233
17. Career Impact: CAPA as a Professional Risk Zone 234
18. From CAPA Closure to CAPA Learning 234
19. The Regulator's Unspoken Expectation 234
20. Final Reflection: CAPA Is Where Trust Is Earned 235

Conclusion 237
The Audit Was Never the Real Problem 237
Why Traditional Quality Systems Struggle Today 238
Artificial Intelligence as a Structural Response, Not a Trend 239
The Central Theme: Visibility Before Control 240
Risk Management Revisited: From Forms to Awareness 240
CAPA: Where Systems Reveal Their True Maturity 241
Data Integrity: The Silent Backbone 242
Governance: The Line Between Support and Liability 243
The Human Role Has Never Been More Important 243
Career Impact: The Unspoken Reality 244
From Audit Survival to Audit Confidence 245
The Regulator's Perspective, Reconsidered 245

The Ethical Dimension 246
A Quiet but Profound Shift 247
Final Reflection 247
Bibliography 249
Regulatory & Inspection Authorities 250
International Standards & Quality Systems 251
World Health Organization (WHO) 252
Artificial Intelligence & Governance 252

About the Author

Amit Kumar Guru is a senior pharmaceutical quality and compliance professional with over two and a half decades of hands-on experience across regulated drug manufacturing, global regulatory inspections, and enterprise quality systems. His career spans the full pharmaceutical product lifecycle, including R&D, manufacturing, quality control, quality assurance, validation, and regulatory compliance, with direct exposure to both innovator and generic environments.

He has worked extensively within highly regulated GxP frameworks, supporting organizations through US FDA, EMA, MHRA, WHO, MCC, TGA, HPFB, PMDA and other international regulatory inspections, and has been directly involved in inspection readiness programs, remediation of critical observations, and long-term quality system transformation initiatives. He worked with various organizations like Ranbaxy Lab Ltd, Cipla Ltd, Merck KgA, Macleods Pharma, Strides Arcolab, Daichi Sankyo, Sunpharma, Sparta Systems, Honeywell & Connexo Co. Ltd. His experience includes leadership roles in electronic Quality Management Systems (eQMS), computerized system validation (CSV), data integrity remediation, and global quality harmonization programs.

Over the years, Amit Kumar Guru has developed a strong reputation for his pragmatic, regulator-aligned approach—bridging the gap between regulatory expectations and operational realities on the shop floor. Rather than treating compliance as a documentation exercise, his work emphasizes system design, governance, accountability, and sustainability, ensuring that quality systems function effectively under real-world conditions.

In recent years, his focus has expanded to the responsible adoption of artificial intelligence and advanced analytics in pharmaceutical environments. He has been closely involved in evaluating how AI, machine learning, and digital technologies can be deployed without compromising data integrity, validation principles, or patient safety. His work in this area is grounded not in technology enthusiasm, but in a deep understanding of regulatory science, risk management, and inspection behavior.

Amit Kumar Guru is a strong advocate for human-centered, risk-based AI adoption, where intelligent systems augment scientific and quality decision-making while preserving transparency, explainability, and regulatory accountability. He regularly advises leadership teams on AI governance models, validation strategies, and cultural readiness, helping organizations transition from traditional compliance models to future-ready, digitally enabled quality systems.

This book reflects the belief that artificial intelligence in pharmaceutical quality is not a race for innovation, but a discipline of responsibility. It argues that AI does not solve compliance problems; it reveals whether quality systems truly understand themselves. Positioned not as a technological upgrade but as a catalyst for regulatory maturity, the book emphasizes that sustainable audit confidence is built through visibility rather than documentation volume. It reinforces that real risk management is continuous, CAPA effectiveness defines organizational credibility more than closure, and governance—not algorithms—determines whether AI becomes an asset or a liability. Rejecting hype in favor of regulatory realism, the work presents artificial intelligence as a support for professional judgment rather than a substitute for GMP thinking, asserting that audits are reflections of system awareness, not adversarial events. Ultimately, it conveys the conviction that artificial intelligence delivers meaningful value in pharmaceuticals only when it strengthens quality culture, regulatory trust, leadership accountability, and long-term professional integrity.

Acknowledgement

This book is offered with deep gratitude and respect to the people whose influence shaped both my values and my journey.

It is dedicated first to the memory of my father, **Late Mr. H. N. Guru**, whose life embodied discipline, integrity, and quiet strength.

His belief in responsibility over recognition continues to guide every professional decision I make.

I also dedicate this work to my mother, **Late Mrs. Vidya Guru**, whose resilience, patience, and moral clarity formed the foundation of my character.

Her faith in learning and perseverance remains my enduring source of strength.

Together, my parents taught me that true success is measured not by achievement, but by conduct.

I acknowledge with sincere appreciation my uncle, **Mr. B. L. Mishra**, for his steady guidance and unwavering encouragement.

His perspective and support provided stability during critical phases of both life and career.

I am deeply grateful to my elder brother, **Dr. Vineet Guru**, whose academic rigor and intellectual discipline set a benchmark I continue to aspire toward.

His example reinforced the importance of depth, accuracy, and lifelong learning.

I express my sincere gratitude to **Mr. Shawn Lee**, CEO & Founder of **Connexo Co. Ltd.**, for his invaluable support and encouragement during the writing of this book.

His visionary leadership and deep understanding of quality, compliance, and digital transformation in the pharmaceutical industry served as a constant source of inspiration.

The insights shared by him helped shape the practical relevance and industry alignment of this work.

His belief in innovation-driven quality systems reinforced the core philosophy presented in this book.

I am especially thankful for his guidance, constructive feedback, and motivation throughout the journey.

Mr. Shawn Lee's commitment to excellence and future-ready solutions greatly influenced the direction of this content.

This book carries reflections of his forward-thinking approach toward regulated industries.

I sincerely appreciate the time and trust he extended during the development of this manuscript.

His support made this intellectual endeavor both meaningful and impactful.

I acknowledge his contribution with deep respect and gratitude.

I would like to express my deepest gratitude to Dr. Uday Rakibe & Pharmamantra Quality Learners Team for his invaluable guidance, wisdom, and unwavering support throughout my journey. His insights and experience have played a pivotal role in shaping my understanding of AI in the pharmaceutical domain. I am truly fortunate to have learned under his mentorship, which has greatly influenced this work.

I would like to sincerely acknowledge Mr. Ranjit Barshikar for his exceptional contributions and thought leadership in the field of pharmaceutical quality and compliance. His deep expertise and forward-thinking perspective have been a constant source of inspiration while shaping this work. I am truly grateful for his guidance and the impact it has had on my journey in AI within pharma.

I would like to express my sincere gratitude to Mr. Vijay Kshirsagar for his valuable guidance and unwavering support throughout my journey. His practical insights and depth of experience have significantly contributed to my understanding of the pharmaceutical domain. I am truly thankful for his mentorship, which has meaningfully influenced this work on AI in Pharma.

I extend my thanks to my professional colleague, Ms. Madhulika Mishra, for her collaboration, insight, and thoughtful engagement.

Her professional integrity and clarity of thought contributed meaningfully to my work and reflections.

I sincerely appreciate support from my family members Mrs. Preeti Mishra, Mr. Shiv Kumar Mishra, Mrs. Vibha Guru, Mrs. Keerti Dubey, Mr. Manish Dubey, Mr. Anmol Dubey, Ms. Mahak Mishra, Ms. Aaradhya Guru.

I express my sincere appreciation to Mr. Shaleen Mishra for his editorial insight, structural guidance, and disciplined approach to refining this work.

His ability to align complex ideas with clarity and coherence significantly strengthened the final manuscript.

I am equally grateful to Mr. Peeyush Guru, Ms. Rajeshwari Mishra & Ms. Sonali Mishra for their meticulous review, thoughtful feedback, and attention to detail throughout the editorial process.

Their perspective helped ensure precision, consistency, and balance across the content.

Their combined editorial contributions played a vital role in shaping the quality and integrity of this book.

I am also thankful for adroit guidance and prompt support for my mentors and colleagues Dr. Subhash Deshpande, Mr. Jin Kim, Ms. Hanna Hwang, Dr. Deo Narain Dixit, Dr Jayant Karajgi, Mr. Deepak Kasbi, Mr. Deepak Haldhankar, Mr. Digambar Nigade, Mr. Alvin Ng, Mr. Rajendra Dadhich, Mr. Vipul Joshi, Mr Sushil Jaiswal, Mr. Vijay Agarwal, Mr. Dhananjay Vishwakarma, Mr. Nilesh Kshirsagar, Mr. Pranav Gadre, Mr. Arabindakashaya Mishra, Mr. Ashutosh Mittal, Mr. Asit Das, Mr Sandeep Bharadwaj, Mr. Bhupesh Soni, Mr. Ajay Dasoondi, Mr. Arjun Dasoondi, Mr. Ajay Verma, Mr. Preet Swaroop, Mr. Sandeep Patil, Dr. D S Pandey, Mr. Dale Adkisson, Mr. Sankalp Dixit, Mr. Vipul Yamdagni, Mr. Sanjay Goswami, Mr. Suresh Jain, Mr. Sanjay Barhate, Mr. Rishabh Ruia, Ms. Matilda George, Mr. Sanjay Jangir, Mr. Biju Mathew, Mr. C K Sundhar, Mr. Braj Kishor Tiwari, Mr. Goutam Saha, Mr. Manish Sharma, Mr. Atul Verma, Mr. Narendra Singh Panwar, Dr. Rakesh Jatav, Mr. Sanjay Merotha, Ms. Tamanna Mehtani, Mr. Hemant Khair, Mr. Rizwan Khan, Ms. Seema Kapasia, Ms. Payal Soni, Mr. Akash Jain, Mr. Sachin Gupta, Mr. Manmohan Sharma, Mrs. Kousthmani Kamath, Dr. Meena Tiwari, Dr. T R Saini, Dr. Rajesh Maheshwari, Mr. Sanjay Jain, Mr. Prabhas Jatav, Mr. Umesh Kale, Mr. Sridhar S. Rao, Mr. Vinay Verma, Mr. Mohit Pateriya, Mr. Neeraj Choudhary, Dr. Anshul Gangele, Mr. Rajneesh Pachauri, Mr. Pratik Jain, Mr. Amit Chaturvedi, Mr. Amitabh Narang, Mr. Bhushan Pawar, Mr. Pradeep Singh, Mr. Vinay Golandaj, Mr Rajiv Tripathi, Mr. Satish Babu, Mr. Manoj Jain, Mr. Om Prakash Kosthi, Dr JP Khuarana, Mr. Ashish Vaidya, Mr. Mangesh Mantri, Mr. Mangesh Honwad, Mr. B M Kulkarni, Mr. Prabir Paul, Mr. Sajarao Gaonkar, Mr. Manoj Sagwekr,

Mr. Sanjit Singh Lamba, Mr. Praveen Kulkarni, Mr Amit Nayak, Mr. Ved Prakash, Mr. Ajit Manocha, Mr. Raghunath Reddy, Mr. Manish Kishore, Mr. Jaiprasad Naidu, Mr. Sunilraj Othena. Each of these individuals influenced this book in ways both visible and unseen.

Their values shaped the way problems are approached, risks are assessed, and responsibility is understood. This book reflects lessons learned long before it was written. It carries forward principles of accountability, humility, and diligence instilled over many years. The support received was not always spoken, but it was always present.

The encouragement offered was not always directive, but it was always steady.

The guidance given was not prescriptive, but it was always principled.

This work stands on foundations built through trust, patience, and example.

It is as much a reflection of those influences as it is of professional experience.

I remain conscious that no work of this nature is created in isolation. Every page carries the

imprint of shared values and collective support.

I am grateful for the freedom to think, the discipline to execute, and the responsibility to deliver.

This acknowledgement is a small expression of a much larger debt.

It recognizes contributions that extend beyond professional boundaries.

It honors relationships grounded in respect rather than expectation.

It reflects gratitude without obligation, and remembrance without loss.

This book is written with awareness of those who made it possible.

It is offered with humility and sincere appreciation.

When Compliance Became Too Complex for Spreadsheets

No regulatory finding ever says, *"You did not use Artificial Intelligence."*

What it says is:

- *You failed to detect a trend.*
- *You did not demonstrate effectiveness.*
- *You could not justify your decision with data.*

The uncomfortable truth is that most pharmaceutical quality failures today are not caused by missing data. They are caused by **not seeing what the data was already saying**.

For decades, human judgment has been the backbone of pharmaceutical decision-making. And rightly so. But the volume, velocity, and interconnectedness of modern quality data have reached a point where judgment alone—unsupported by advanced analysis—creates invisible risk.

This is not a technology problem.

It is a **scale problem**.

The Industry's Unspoken Transition

The pharmaceutical industry has never resisted technology. It has resisted **technology that cannot be controlled**.

Every accepted innovation—electronic batch records, validated systems, computerized QMS platforms—earned its place only after it proved reliability, traceability, and regulatory defensibility.

Artificial Intelligence is now walking that same path.

Not loudly.

Not recklessly.

But cautiously, behind the scenes—inside quality reviews, deviation trending, signal detection, and management oversight discussions.

AI did not arrive because the industry wanted innovation.

It arrived because **manual analysis stopped being sufficient**.

A Question Every Inspector Already Asks

Imagine an inspection room.

An investigator asks for:

- Five years of deviation trends
- Evidence that CAPAs actually reduced recurrence
- Cross-product impact of repeated root causes
- Scientific justification for decisions made months—or years—earlier

The data exists.

But it lives in different systems, formats, and mental models.

What is being evaluated in that moment is not effort.

It is **control over complexity**.

This is where organizations quietly struggle—not due to non-compliance, but due to **cognitive overload**.

Why This Moment Is Different

Regulatory expectations have changed—even if the language has not.

Today's regulators expect:

- Risk-based reasoning, not reactive explanations
- Trend-based insights, not static summaries
- Data integrity at scale, not at sample level

Human-only analysis was never designed for this level of complexity.

And when complexity exceeds human capacity, risk does not disappear.

It becomes **harder to see**.

That is the space AI is beginning to occupy—not as a decision-maker, but as a **decision amplifier**.

What This Book Refuses to Do

This book does not sell AI as a shortcut.

It does not suggest bypassing validation.

It does not claim machines can replace accountability.

There is no "AI will fix compliance" promise here.

Because compliance has never been fixed by tools alone.

What This Book Is Really About

This book is about:

- How AI fits *inside* GxP, not outside it
- Where AI strengthens—not weakens—quality systems
- How explainability, validation, and governance make AI inspectable
- Why leadership decisions, not algorithms, determine success

This is not a book about the future of pharmaceuticals.

It is about what is **already happening**, quietly and cautiously, inside regulated environments—whether acknowledged or not.

Why Chapter One Starts Now

Because AI in pharmaceuticals is not a technology story.

It is a **quality story**.

A **governance story**.

An **accountability story**.

And those stories always begin when the old ways stop scaling—long before anyone admits they have.

Chapter 1

The Audit Fear Nobody Talks About

The Quietest Room in the Plant

You know the room well. It is the small, windowless conference room that suddenly becomes headquarters for every manager, QA lead, and subject-matter expert the night before an inspection officially begins. Coffee goes cold, laptops overheat, and nobody wants to speak above a whisper.

I have sat in that room dozens of times—sometimes as the senior quality lead, sometimes as the external consultant called in to "stress-test" the readiness package. The feeling is always the same: a low-grade dread that the inspector will discover something we have all missed, something that will unravel months of preparation in minutes.

That emotion—persistent, unspoken, yet universally familiar in our industry—is what I call the Audit Fear Nobody Talks About. It is not embarrassment, nor is it a simple worry about failing a compliance hurdle. It is a deeper fear that the very systems we have sworn by, invested in, and proudly described as "robust" will show their true fragility when the inspector starts asking questions none of us rehearsed.

Why does this fear remain unspoken, even among colleagues who have attended the same trainings and shared the same war stories? In this chapter we will name it, dissect it, and examine why the traditional ways of coping (checklists, mock audits, marathon documentation reviews) do not put it to rest. Only when you understand the real source of the fear can you judge, calmly and rationally, where AI-enabled assistance fits in—and more importantly, where it does not.

1. Anatomy of an Unspoken Fear

Fear is rarely born overnight. The kind we feel about audits is a slow brew of four ingredients that mix invisibly into daily operations.

1. The Volume Paradox
   Each year we accumulate more documents, more data points, and more interconnected systems. Ironically, the more we record "for traceability," the harder it becomes for any human to trace anything in real time. We sense that we can no longer personally vouch for every piece of evidence an inspector may request.
2. The Illusion of Synchronized Understanding
   Your manufacturing supervisor, your QC reviewer, and you might use the same SOP titles but hold subtly different mental pictures of what "as per procedure" really means. During normal operations the mismatch stays hidden. In an audit, a single question about responsibility or data review cascades into contradictory answers—and the room temperature drops ten degrees.
3. The Memory Gap
   You remember what went wrong last audit and can recite the corrective actions. What you cannot recall—because nobody can—is every deviation discussion, risk assessment, or equipment log entry that occurred since then. The fear is knowing that the inspector might land on the single forgotten detail.

4. The Inspector's Asymmetry
   Inspectors are trained observers who enter with no operational baggage. They are free to see patterns where insiders see routine. We fear their fresh eyes because our own have grown too accustomed to the plant's quirks.

Notice that none of these ingredients is inherently about bad intent or negligence. They are structural realities of modern pharmaceutical operations. Yet together they seed the fear that "something is hiding in plain sight."

2. From Fear to Audit Failure: The Causal Chain

Let us trace how the unspoken fear can convert into tangible findings, 483 observations, or even Warning Letters.

Stage 1: Hyper-Controlled Preparation
Teams run regimented document drills and pre-approve talking points. In doing so, they often force complexity into tidy boxes, ignoring edge cases to reduce rehearsal time.

Stage 2: Real-Time Scramble
When the inspector requests lineage for a batch or clarification on a change control closed six months ago, the existing rehearsed scripts fracture. Colleagues look for files, email each other mid-audit, and hope the right attachment lands before the next break. Each minute of silence amplifies the inspector's curiosity.

Stage 3: Conflicting Narratives
Because data sources are scattered—ERP tables, LIMS records, unofficial Excel trackers—different staff consult different fragments. Their answers differ enough that the inspector checks whether data integrity controls are effective.

Stage 4: Finding and Expansion
The inspector records a single discrepancy: a mismatch between a material expiration date in LIMS and the date written on the batch record. That point becomes a shovel to dig deeper. The inspection scope widens; the mood in the quiet room turns to dread.

Stage 5: Official Action
A 483 lands. Or worse, a Warning Letter months later references "systemic failure to ensure data accuracy and consistency." The original fear has materialized into a public document accessible to competitors, partners, and investors.

Notice the irony: it was not the initial discrepancy that harmed the company most—it was how the scramble exposed a pattern that might have remained invisible had the team possessed a real-time, consolidated view.

3. Traditional Coping Mechanisms—and Why They Fall Short

Over the past twenty years, I have seen five standard responses to audit fear. Each was logical at the time; each eventually proved insufficient.

1. The Binder Wall
   Teams assemble "Day-1 Binders" so thick they require their own dolly. These binders create a comforting illusion: everything an inspector could ask is captured in one place. But pharmaceutical operations evolve daily; by the time the inspector arrives, at least a few documents are outdated.
2. The All-Hands Drill
   Staff perform mock inspections, peppering colleagues with rapid-fire questions. These drills are valuable for muscle

memory but frequently focus on known questions, not the novel pivots true inspectors employ.

3. The Documentation Sprint
   Two weeks before the audit, every department races to close open deviations and CAPAs. The closure quality often drops, signaling to a savvy inspector that the organization manages quality by calendar, not by risk.
4. The Expert Firewall
   A select "audit team" intercepts all inquiries, filtering them before engaging operators. Effective on simple clerical requests, this approach backfires when inspectors ask to speak with the person who performed the work.
5. The Last-Minute Consultant
   Companies bring in outside experts (people like me) to perform pre-inspections. These reviews highlight gaps but rarely allow time for systemic fixes; instead, teams patch localized issues, leaving the underlying disarray untouched.

The weakness in every coping mechanism is time compression. All energy is invested in the short window before or during the audit, when risk visibility needs to be continuous, not episodic.

4. Where AI-Assisted Visibility Changes the Game

Let me be precise: AI does not cure fear, nor does it guarantee a clean audit. What it can do—if correctly framed—is provide a "continuous nervous system" that surfaces weak signals long before an inspector visits. The benefits flow in three dimensions.

Early Warning on Pattern Deviations
Machine-learning classification models can monitor deviations in real time, clustering similar root causes across departments. You

are alerted when a pattern emerges—say, an uptick in "equipment calibration missing" deviations across multiple lines—even if no single deviation looks alarming. Humans can then intervene before the cluster hardens into a systemic weakness.

Contextual Document Mapping
Natural-language algorithms can cross-reference batch records, SOPs, and change controls to spot mismatches in terminology or outdated references. Rather than flipping binders, you receive a heat-map of documents that need harmonization.

Confidence Scoring for Data Integrity
Rule-based AI checks whether raw data, metadata, and reported values align across systems (e.g., LIMS vs. SCADA). When confidence drops below a threshold, the batch is flagged for manual inspection long before release.

These capabilities shift the timeline: instead of discovering issues during an audit scramble, you can address them during routine operations, shrinking the unknown unknowns that feed fear.

5. Common Mistakes When Reaching for Technology

Because the fear is intense, managers sometimes rush into tech adoption that recreates the very fragility they hoped to eliminate. Watch for these pitfalls:

- Automating the Unknown
  Installing AI dashboards without first mapping existing data flows results in dashboards that scream false alarms or, worse, stay silent.
- Treating AI as Black-Box Guru
  Some see AI recommendations as orders. Remember,

regulators expect you—not an algorithm—to justify actions. Always keep a human layer of critical judgment.

- Over-Indexing on KPIs
  Teams enamored with colorful metrics might ignore small data anomalies that lack glamour but hold critical compliance relevance.
- Ignoring Data Hygiene
  AI amplifies underlying data quality. Feed it erroneous timestamps, and you'll get elegantly wrong insights. Dedicate resources to data integrity before expecting automation magic.
- Neglecting Change-Management
  Rolling out new tech two weeks before an inspection confuses staff and suggests to inspectors that the system is unvalidated. Build adoption gradually and document the validation rigorously.

6. The "Continuous Transparency" Framework

Over the years I have refined a practical model for diffusing audit fear. It is technology-agnostic, but certain AI capabilities fit naturally within it.

Step 1: Map Your Risk Hotspots
Identify processes where data volume, human intervention, and regulatory scrutiny converge—often deviations, batch release, and third-party data exchange.

Step 2: Establish Real-Time Visibility
Implement dashboards that track these hotspots daily, not monthly. For manual processes, use simple checklists first; automation can layer on top later.

Step 3: Design Multi-Source Correlation
Ensure that your visibility layer reconciles information from different systems. This is where AI text-matching or statistical checks shine—linking the maintenance log to the deviation record to the CAPA tracker.

Step 4: Define Alert Logic with Humans in Control
Choose thresholds based on risk tolerance set by your Quality Council. Alerts must route to accountable owners, not just appear as red dots on a screen.

Step 5: Audit-Trail the Resolution
Every time the system flags an issue, capture what investigation occurred, what evidence was reviewed, and how conclusions were drawn. This record itself becomes potent audit evidence.

Step 6: Iterate and Educate
Hold monthly retrospectives: did the system flag meaningful issues? Did staff act in time? Is threshold tuning needed? Use these sessions to educate rather than blame.

By progressing through these steps, you move fear into structured awareness, turning the unknown into the known and the unseen into the tracked.

7. Field Story: The Calibration Catastrophe That Never Happened

Allow me to share a case—a mid-size sterile injectables manufacturer in the U.S. Midwest. Two years earlier, they had barely survived an FDA inspection, receiving five 483 observations mainly centered on data integrity. Determined to improve, they adopted a continuous transparency approach.

They started by feeding historical deviation data—3,200 records spanning five years—into a simple clustering algorithm.

Patterns emerged: equipment calibration issues peaked roughly every thirteen months, aligned with seasonal staff changes. Armed with this knowledge, the team revised the calibration schedule, introduced cross-training, and set up automated reminders via their maintenance system.

Sixteen months later, an FDA inspector asked precisely about equipment calibration during sterile fill operations. The team produced not only the updated calendar but also a trend chart showing how deviation frequency had dropped 78% since the process change. The inspector smiled: "Good to see proactive management." No observation was issued.

The calamity—an inevitable discrepancy on an uncalibrated instrument—never occurred because weak signals had been caught early. That is the quiet power of AI when used as a decision-support layer.

8. Mistake Autopsies: Learning from Pain

Not every company fares as well. Here are condensed autopsies of common AI-related missteps:

- Overfitting to Past Audits
  One firm trained its models solely on deviations that triggered observations in the previous inspection cycle. The system ignored emerging risks (e.g., remote data transfer validation) because they lacked historical precedent. Result: a new class of findings blindsided them.
- Untested Update
  Another plant pushed a model upgrade days before an EMA inspection. The model crashed under load, eliminating the trending dashboard the team had showcased in opening

presentations. Inspectors noted "lack of validated systems for real-time monitoring."

- Governance Vacuum
  A third site gave IT ownership of the AI platform but failed to integrate QA oversight. Data security patches were delayed; access logs went unread. MHRA inspectors identified privilege escalations, concluding that the company did not "maintain appropriate control over quality-related computerized systems."

Patterns are clear: technology loudness cannot substitute for disciplined governance.

9. Practical Mindset Shift: From Gatekeeping to Storytelling

Think of an upcoming audit as a storytelling exercise. An inspector wants to hear the narrative of how your product remains safe, pure, and effective throughout its lifecycle. Every dataset, document, and conversation should align to that plot.

Gatekeeping mindsets—hiding data or hoping the right question is never asked—come from fear. Continuous transparency, augmented by AI, empowers storytelling. Instead of waiting to be challenged, you present an evolving narrative backed by living data. The inspector's questions become chapter prompts, not ambushes.

When you adopt this mindset, AI tools transform from cryptic machines into narrative aids. A predictive deviation chart is merely your plot twist detector. A document consistency checker is your continuity editor. You remain the author.

10. Key Takeaways

- The "Audit Fear Nobody Talks About" stems from volume, hidden complexity, memory gaps, and inspector asymmetry—not from laziness or incompetence.
- Traditional coping strategies fail because they compress risk management into the audit window instead of embedding it into daily operations.
- Properly governed AI can provide early warning on pattern deviations, contextual document mapping, and data-integrity confidence scoring—reducing unknowns that fuel fear.
- Common pitfalls include treating AI as a black box, neglecting data hygiene, and bypassing change-management rigor.
- Adopt a Continuous Transparency Framework: map hotspots, establish real-time visibility, correlate data, maintain human-controlled alerts, audit-trail resolutions, and iterate.
- Shift from a gatekeeping to a storytelling mindset, where every piece of data supports a coherent narrative of product quality.

Confronting the fear openly is the first act in your audit survival journey. In the next chapter, we will explore a painful truth many companies discover too late: "We Were Compliant… On Paper." Understanding that gap sets the stage for deciding where manual compliance is faltering and how intelligent automation can lend real muscle to our systems.

Chapter 2

We Were Compliant... On Paper

A Curious Compliment

An FDA investigator once paid me what sounded like a compliment.

"Your documentation is immaculate," she said, closing the last of eight binders on my conference-room table. Then she added, almost as an afterthought: "Now let's see if any of it is true."

That single sentence explains why this chapter exists. Most pharmaceutical sites I visit believe they are compliant because their paper trail says so. The audit findings that follow—Form 483 citations, warning letters, import alerts—demonstrate a harsher reality: immaculate paperwork does not guarantee compliant operations. In fact, it can hide non-compliance so well that nobody sees it until an inspector does.

In Chapter 1 we talked about the unspoken fear that keeps quality professionals awake at night. Now we turn the spotlight on the source of that fear: the widening gap between documented intent and operational reality. If you have ever felt both proud and uneasy while handing an SOP to an auditor, this chapter is for you.

1. The Illusion of "Binder Compliance"

If you credibly document a procedure, train personnel, and archive the records, regulators call that good practice. Over time, however, documentation can morph into a comfort blanket:

- Procedures get copied into new SOPs without verifying that they still match the shop floor.
- Deviations are closed with elegant root-cause diagrams but minimal shop-floor change.
- Annual product quality reviews (APQRs) highlight the same "opportunities" year after year.

The result is an organization that is compliant—on paper. The real-world system has drifted, pixel by pixel, away from what the paperwork describes.

I call this drift the "Compliance Mirage." Like a desert mirage, it appears convincing until you step closer.

2. Where the Mirage Comes From

1. Procedural Debt

Every procedure captures a moment in time: a particular piece of equipment, a specific skill set, a production cadence. The moment the ink dries, reality starts to move on. Production output increases. Operators rotate. Equipment parameters are tweaked. None of these changes is malicious; they are simply how living systems evolve. Yet each unrecorded tweak becomes procedural debt—a gap between the documented process and the practiced one. Eventually the debt balloons into systemic risk.

2. Cosmetic CAPAs

Regulators encourage Corrective and Preventive Actions (CAPAs), but they also notice when CAPAs solve paperwork more than problems. A common pattern:

Deviation raised → SOP rewritten → training record signed → deviation closed.

Nothing on the floor physically changes, so the same deviation reappears under a new ticket number. The CAPA system becomes a camouflaging mechanism.

3. Siloed Data Landscapes

Batch records live in one system, environmental monitoring in another, and maintenance logs in spreadsheets on a supervisor's laptop. Individually each record passes muster; collectively they tell conflicting stories—a batch accepted despite HVAC alarms, bioburden spikes ignored because nobody correlated them. With no way to stitch the narratives together, quality reviewers assume harmony where discord exists.

4. Psychological Safety Nets

Humans crave closure and certainty. A stamped, approved document offers both. It says: "We thought about this; therefore, we controlled it." Over time teams learn to equate documents with control, and the absence of documents with risk. Real-world signals that contradict the document are subconsciously downgraded—"That can't be important; otherwise, it would be in the SOP."

3. How the Mirage Trips Audits

Inspectors do not judge you by the beauty of your documents; they judge you by the alignment between documents and reality. Here is the typical unmasking sequence:

1. They read the SOP.
2. They watch the operator perform the task.
3. They ask for supporting data (logs, trends, equipment screens).
4. They cross-reference the three sources.

Any mismatch lights up like a red flag. Once one flag appears, the investigator's mindset shifts: "If they missed this, what else did they miss?" That curiosity soon expands the scope of the audit, sometimes from a single deviation to a full systems investigation.

Let me illustrate with a real (anonymized) example.

4. Case Study: The Cleanroom That Failed in the Database

A sterile injectables facility prided itself on pristine cleanrooms. The gowning SOP was fourteen pages, complete with step-by-step photos. Training records showed every operator had passed gowning qualification, and daily logbooks were filled diligently.

During an EMA inspection, the investigator compared particle counts in the Environmental Monitoring (EM) database with gowning events. A pattern emerged: spikes in particles within 10 minutes after specific operators entered the room—operators who, according to records, were fully qualified.

The finding? Gowning technique drifted over time. Operators were skipping one subtle glove-disinfection step that did not appear in the training video but still existed in the SOP. The EM trend, not the binder, told the story. The facility received a Major Observation for "failure to ensure gowning procedures are consistently followed," spawning requalification and weeks of production delay.

The site was compliant on paper, yet non-compliant in practice.

5. Why Traditional Fixes Fail

More SOPs, More Templates

When gaps show up, the instinct is to write another SOP or add another form field. This helps you feel proactive, but it also adds cognitive load. Operators already juggling ten checklists now juggle twelve. Complexity becomes its own source of error.

Manual Cross-Checks

Quality units often deploy "intensive data reviews." A team member manually reconciles batch records with logbooks and equipment prints. The process is slow, retrospective, and subject to reviewer fatigue. Errors slip through or are discovered weeks after release, too late to prevent shipment of non-conforming product.

Periodic Internal Audits

Self-inspections are valuable, yet they occur quarterly or annually. By the time an internal audit discovers a gap, thousands of vials may already be in commerce. Moreover, internal auditors share the same organizational blind spots as the people they audit. You cannot see what you all unconsciously ignore.

6. Where AI and Automation Help—Without the Hype

Artificial intelligence will not magically make people follow procedures, and it will never own the GMP responsibility. What it can do is illuminate the drift before an inspector does. Think of AI as a continuously running alignment engine, comparing three realities:

1. What the procedure says should happen.
2. What the data shows actually happened.
3. How the historical pattern behaved when everything was demonstrably in control.

When any of those realities deviate beyond a risk-based threshold, the system nudges you—daily, not during the next annual review.

Practical Applications

- Contextual Alerts: Instead of a generic alarm, the system indicates, "Glove disinfection step skipped based on camera inference; EM trend risk increased 32%."
- Pattern Correlation: It correlates HVAC parameters, particle counts, and operator ID without you manually merging datasets.
- Living SOP Analytics: When the same deviation type recurs, the platform suggests that a procedural step may be unclear, prompting preventive rewriting rather than cosmetic fixes.

Notice what the AI is not doing: rewriting SOPs, deciding product disposition, or bypassing human judgment. It merely surfaces patterns that paper alone cannot reveal.

7. Common Missteps When Digitizing Compliance

1. Automation Without Process Understanding
   It is tempting to overlay fancy analytics on a flawed process. If sampling frequency is wrong, statistical power will be weak no matter how advanced the algorithm.
2. Data Swamps
   Collecting everything "just in case" creates unusable lakes of semi-structured data. AI relies on signal quality; garbage in, garbage out remains a timeless principle.
3. Over-Confidence in Dashboards
   Visual dashboards look authoritative. Teams sometimes trust the green checkmark over their own shop-floor intuition. A balanced culture respects both human observation and machine insight.

4. Ignoring the Human Feedback Loop
   Operators must understand why the system flagged their action. Without contextual feedback, they see alerts as nuisances and invent workarounds—often by disabling the alert.
5. Treating AI Findings as Deviations
   Every AI-generated anomaly need not become a deviation record. A triage framework is essential; otherwise, you flood the QMS and recreate the very paperwork burden you wanted to escape.

8. The Living Compliance Pyramid: A Framework

To bridge the gap between paper and practice, I teach teams a three-layer model.

1. Foundational Layer – Documented Intent
   The SOP, batch record, risk assessment, and validation protocol define what "good" looks like. Without this layer, the pyramid collapses.
2. Operational Layer – Executed Reality
   This is the bloodstream of data: equipment tags, SCADA logs, human observations, LIMS results. It must be captured where it happens, when it happens.
3. Alignment Layer – Continuous Reconciliation
   AI lives here. It reconciles intent and reality daily, highlighting divergences at the earliest plausible moment. Humans then decide: correct, refine, or document the difference.

When all three layers communicate, compliance ceases to be a snapshot and becomes a living, breathing state. Paperwork still matters, but it no longer blinds you to drift.

9. Mindset Shift: From Narrative to Evidence

Ask yourself whenever you update a procedure: "How will we know if this step stops happening three months from now?" If the answer is "Because the operator signs the form," you are staring at a compliance mirage. Develop an evidence plan: What data will prove this step occurred? How will that data reach someone who can act on it within 24 hours? When you think this way, AI is not an add-on; it is part of the evidence plan.

10. Key Takeaways

- Documentation is necessary but not sufficient; alignment between documents and operations determines audit outcomes.
- Procedural debt, cosmetic CAPAs, siloed data, and psychological safety nets fuel the Compliance Mirage.
- Traditional controls—more SOPs, manual reviews, periodic audits—struggle against real-time drift.
- AI excels at continuous reconciliation, correlating disparate data streams to expose divergence early.
- Automation must be risk-based, data-quality-minded, and tightly integrated with human decision loops.
- Adopt the Living Compliance Pyramid: Documented Intent, Executed Reality, Continuous Reconciliation.
- Design procedures with an evidence plan, ensuring every critical step leaves a data footprint that surfaces in near real time.

Looking Ahead

Now that we have dismantled the fiction of "paper equals compliance," you may wonder how auditors spot the cracks so quickly. What cues do they follow? What mental models do they use to decide whether to trust you? In Chapter 3—"How Inspectors Actually Think"—we will walk inside an auditor's mindset and learn how to anticipate their questions before they ask them.

Chapter 3

How Inspectors Actually Think

Welcome Back—From Paper Reality to the Inspector's Reality

In the last chapter we saw how a site can look immaculate on paper yet still unravel in front of an inspector. You and I both know that maddening moment: the documents are perfect, the SOP signatures line up, and still the inspector's eyebrow shoots up after the very first question. Why? Because regulators don't audit paper; they audit confidence, consistency, and genuine process control.

To survive—with careers and reputations intact—we must learn to think like they do. This chapter is about stepping into the inspector's shoes, understanding their cognitive tools, and seeing our facilities through their lens. Once you grasp that worldview, the later discussion on AI and automation will click into place.

1. The Inspector's Mandate: Public Health, Not Paperwork

When an FDA, EMA, or MHRA inspector walks through your security gate, their badge represents more than a government agency. It symbolizes a social contract: medicines must be safe, effective, and of consistent quality. Everything else—documents, data, IT systems, lab instruments—exists to serve that purpose.

An inspector's mental loop typically runs like this:

- If I let this product reach patients, could someone get hurt?

- What could go wrong here that nobody has noticed—or reported—yet?
- How quickly can I gather enough evidence to justify trust or escalate concern?

Those three questions govern every glance at a batch record and every conversation in a conference room. Lose sight of them, and your responses start sounding like defensive legal briefs rather than assurances of patient safety.

2. Risk-Based Triaging: How Limited Time Shapes Their Focus

Inspectors operate under severe time pressure. A routine pre-approval inspection may last five days; a for-cause visit could be three. They cannot possibly review 100 % of your data, so they triage relentlessly. Their first hour on site typically sets a risk map that guides every subsequent sample and question.

Key triage levers:

- Product and process complexity—biologics trump tablets.
- Patient population—oncology injectables draw more scrutiny than topical creams.
- Site history—an old 483 lingers like a shadow in the inspection room.
- Real-time behavior—hesitation, confusion, or conflicting answers accelerate deep dives.

If you feel the inspection shifting suddenly into investigative mode, it likely means those early heuristics signaled elevated risk.

3. The "Smell Test": First Five Minutes, Lasting Impressions

Seasoned inspectors develop an almost visceral sense—a smell test—that tells them whether a site is in control. It starts at reception:

- How many minutes to print my badge?
- Does the escort know the inspection agenda, or is she scrambling?
- Are training records of the inspection team pre-pulled or "being fetched"?
- Tiny cues feed a subconscious trust score. Think of it like a Bayesian prior: a strong first impression biases their belief in your systems; a sloppy welcome makes them expect hidden landmines.

A personal anecdote: During an EMA inspection I supported, the inspector noted that our visitor logbook had two different pens on consecutive entries. He casually asked why. The receptionist admitted one pen had dried out. To us it was trivial; to him it hinted at uncontrolled stationery—a micro-symbol of potential larger control gaps. It set the tone for an aggressive data-integrity deep dive that followed.

4. Building the Story: Inspectors as Investigative Journalists

Contrary to popular myth, inspectors don't merely tick checklists; they construct narratives. Each document, interview, and walk-through either strengthens or weakens the storyline: "This site reliably produces quality product and detects problems before patients do."

Narrative pillars:

1. Process Understanding—Do people grasp *why* each step exists?
2. Data Credibility—Are numbers traceable, untampered, contemporaneously recorded?
3. Management Commitment—Does leadership reinforce quality over output?

If any pillar cracks, the narrative shifts from "in control" to "risk to public health." 483 observations or warning letters are simply the epilogue of a story gone wrong.

5. Cognitive Toolkit: Pattern Recognition, Triangulation, and Outlier Hunting

Inspectors juggle an astonishing amount of multidimensional data. They rely on cognitive shortcuts honed by years of audits.

Pattern Recognition
They have mental libraries of failure modes: forged signatures, backdated entries, unexplained vial breakages. Spot one familiar pattern, and they instinctively probe deeper.

Triangulation
Ask three people the same question in different ways; match answers against records. Misalignment indicates either poor training or deliberate deception—both fatal.

Outlier Hunting
Statistical instinct guides them to outliers in batch yields, deviation frequency, or environmental excursions. An unexplained dip in yield is a neon sign for potential data manipulation.

Recognize these tools, and you can prepare authentic, consistent responses rather than rehearsed scripts that crumble under cross-examination.

6. Why Traditional "Inspection Readiness" Often Fails

Most companies respond to inspection anxiety by forming a war room, printing mountains of binders, and rehearsing Q&A flashcards. This stagecraft calms nerves but rarely fools inspectors. The shortcomings:

- Over-curation—Producing only "happy-path" documents raises suspicion.
- Last-minute clean-ups—Data "reconstructions" leave time-stamp fingerprints.
- Siloed rehearsals—Quality, production, and lab teams practice answers separately, leading to mismatched narratives.

Remember, inspectors look for real-time system control, not theatrical compliance.

7. Inside the Interview Room: Verbal and Non-Verbal Signals

When you sit across the table, an inspector interprets every pause, glance, and throat clear.

What inspectors notice:

- Latency—excessive delay before answering suggests data mining, not recall.
- Qualifiers—phrases like "to the best of my knowledge" ring alarm bells.

- Eye contact—avoiding it may imply uncertainty or concealment.
- Whispering outside the room—signals orchestrated answers.

Being technically correct counts, but being confidently consistent under cross-questioning counts more.

8. Escalation Pathways: From Curiosity to Concern to Compliance Action

Understanding escalation thresholds helps you intercept issues before they snowball.

1. Curiosity—Initial questions to confirm routine controls.
2. Concern—Follow-up probes into anomalies; inspector requests raw data.
3. Verification—Sampling broader datasets, on-the-spot walkthroughs.
4. Evidence Capture—Taking photographs, copying files; now we're in 483 territory.
5. Enforcement—483, Warning Letter, Import Alert, Consent Decree.

Each stage is harder to reverse. Transparency at Stage 2 can prevent a march to Stage 4.

9. Case Study: The Spectrophotometer That Sank a Site

A sterile injectable plant prided itself on a spotless deviation record—only two minor deviations in 18 months. During an FDA inspection, the investigator asked to see UV spectrophotometer calibration logs. An operator produced a Word document printed that morning. The inspector noticed the header "Revision 3" but found no Revision 1 or 2 in the DMS. Further digging revealed the instrument's audit trail had multiple login deletions the night before inspection.

Why did this trigger a Warning Letter? Not because a single log was missing, but because it betrayed four inspector red flags:

- Discrepancy between records (low deviations) and reality (instrument issues).
- Temporal proximity of edits to inspection start.
- Lack of systemic safeguards for audit trails.
- Management unawareness—quality head learned about it at same moment as inspector.

Had the site understood the inspector's risk signals, they might have self-reported, contextualized, and contained the issue. Instead, the inspector concluded, "If they fake calibration, what else are they hiding?"

10. Where AI and Automation Enter the Picture—But Only Later

At this stage you might be itching to know how AI could have saved that sterile plant. Hold that thought. First, we must accept a hard truth: No algorithm can compensate for a culture that conceals problems or a leadership team detached from daily operations.

What AI *can* do—when implemented thoughtfully—is:

- Surface anomalies before humans scramble to fix them retroactively.
- Provide immutable, time-stamped data trails inspectors trust more than Word files.

- Enable consistent, cross-functional visibility so everyone tells the same coherent story.

We'll dig into those capabilities in Part 2, but never forget they supplement, not substitute, the principles we're discussing here.

11. Common Missteps to Avoid When "Reading" Inspectors

1. Assuming silence means approval—Inspectors often reserve judgment until the wrap-up.
2. Over-answering—Volunteering speculative details can open new audit threads.
3. Blaming predecessors—Signals lack of ownership.
4. Quoting regulations verbatim—Comes across as defensive rather than helpful.
5. Using jargon to obscure simplicity—Inspectors cut through acronyms quickly; obfuscation backfires.

12. A Practical Framework: The Credibility Loop

To align with inspector thinking, adopt the Credibility Loop:

1. Declare—State how a process works and why.
2. Demonstrate—Show real-time execution or data.
3. Corroborate—Provide historical evidence and cross-functional confirmation.
4. Reflect—Admit limitations and show improvement actions.

Loop through these steps every time you discuss a procedure. It mirrors the inspector's investigative path and satisfies their need for narrative consistency.

13. Putting It All Together

Why this problem exists

- Companies optimize for passing document reviews, not for genuine process transparency.
- Time-starved inspectors lean on heuristics, making first impressions critical.

How it causes audit failures

- Misalignment between staged readiness and inspector risk triage triggers deeper scrutiny.
- Small inconsistencies snowball into systemic credibility gaps.

Why traditional approaches fail

- War-room theatrics ignore human-factor cues inspectors prioritize.
- Siloed rehearsals crumble under triangulation.

Where AI/automation genuinely helps

- Real-time anomaly detection prevents last-minute data doctoring.
- Immutable audit trails build trust efficiently.

Common mistakes to avoid

- Treating inspectors as adversaries rather than partners in patient safety.
- Equating document volume with assurance.
- Assuming charisma compensates for data gaps.

Mindset or framework

- Adopt the Credibility Loop and reinforce it with a culture that welcomes, rather than fears, transparency.

14. Key Takeaways

- Inspectors audit risk narratives, not binders.
- Their cognitive toolkit—pattern recognition, triangulation, outlier hunting—thrives on inconsistencies.
- First impressions set the Bayesian prior for the entire inspection.
- Traditional "inspection readiness" collapses if people can't answer coherently and consistently.
- AI can support credibility but only when cultural and procedural foundations are solid.

Transition to Part 2

Now that we've stepped into the inspector's head, it's time to examine our own house. In the next chapter we'll dissect why manual, document-heavy compliance models are fraying under modern manufacturing complexity—and why that tension opens the door for thoughtful AI assistance. If you've ever felt crushed by endless spreadsheets and SOP updates, you'll recognize the symptoms. Let's diagnose them together before we prescribe automation.

Chapter 4

Why Manual Compliance Is Breaking Pharma

A Quick Look Back—and a Glimpse Ahead

In the previous chapter we stepped inside an inspector's head. You saw how auditors stitch together fragments of information, probe for weak signals, and mentally run "what-if" simulations of failure modes. That bird's-eye view is essential, but it also exposes a brutal truth: the way most companies still pursue compliance is fundamentally at odds with how inspectors evaluate it.

This chapter is the turning point of the book. Until now we have talked largely about *why* audits fail. From here forward we will explore *what* can be done—realistically, sustainably, and regulator-friendly. To do that, we must first understand why the traditional practice of "manual compliance" is straining, creaking, and in many plants, already snapping. Only then will the logic of AI and automation become obvious rather than hype-driven.

1. The Legacy of Manual Compliance

I still remember my first FDA inspection back in the early 1990s. The plant had a six-drawer metal filing cabinet labeled "Quality Documentation—Current Year." Every month a junior officer would stuff another dossier of batch records, deviation forms, and environmental monitoring logs into it. That cabinet was the heart of our *manual* compliance system.

Fast-forward three decades and many plants still operate on the same fundamental premise:

- People create evidence of compliance.
- That evidence is stored in physical or digital files.
- When an inspector asks, the team retrieves and explains it.

It sounds simple and, in theory, it is. The difference is scale. The volume of data, complexity of supply chains, and velocity of change have exploded, but the mental model—"Write it, file it, retrieve it"—has barely evolved. This mismatch is not an inconvenience. It is a systemic risk.

1.1 How We Got Here

Regulations never mandated paper. They mandated *evidence.* Paper just happened to be the cheapest, most universal medium when GMP rules were written. Even when spreadsheets and electronic document management arrived, the cultural pattern did not shift. We merely swapped filing cabinets for network drives and hoped for the best.

1.2 The Comfort of the Visible

Manual systems give the illusion of control. You can hold a batch record, flip through pages, and check ink signatures. There is tactile satisfaction in seeing documents pile up in archive boxes. Unfortunately, that comfort masks three weaknesses: latency, opacity, and fragility—issues we will visit repeatedly in this chapter.

2. The Hidden Physics of Human Error

Let's be brutally honest. Humans are not designed for high-volume, zero-defect data handling. Cognitive psychology gives us a litany of limitations:

- Working memory caps at about seven items.
- Attention degrades after 20-30 minutes of repetitive work.
- Confirmation bias and fatigue skew observations.

In a GMP context, those limitations manifest as transposed numbers in logbooks, missed signatures, or misinterpreted specifications—exactly the stuff inspectors pounce on.

2.1 Error Propagation in Manual Chains

A line operator writes "23.0 °C" instead of "32.0 °C" in the room log. A supervisor initials without cross-checking. The deviation investigation misses the mismatch because the log is scanned as a PDF and stored. Months later an auditor spots the discrepancy. That single slip evaporates confidence in every temperature-sensitive batch produced that week.

Manual compliance is brittle because every data hand-off is a potential fracture point. The more steps, the higher the compound probability of failure.

3. Compliance Debt: The Quiet Accumulation of Risk

Software engineers talk about "technical debt"—shortcuts that speed release today but cause compounding pain later. In quality management we accumulate something similar: compliance debt.

Every time we:

- extend a spreadsheet template instead of validating a system,
- postpone a root-cause analysis because quarters close, or
- add yet another checklist to patch a gap,

we borrow time against future inspections. Like any debt, the interest eventually exceeds the principal.

3.1 Recognizing the Symptoms

Compliance debt rarely appears on dashboards. You feel it in hallway conversations:

"Did we ever reconcile those calibration certificates?"

"Where's the latest supplier audit report?"

"Who has access to the raw HPLC files?"

When those questions surface during routine operations, imagine the tension when an inspector asks them under oath.

4. Audit-Time Shock: When Manual Systems Freeze

Picture the scene: Day two of a European Medicines Agency inspection. The assessor asks for the complete chain of custody for a critical API sample, including raw equipment files, not just the transcribed results. Five people scatter to different rooms. Three hours pass. The atmosphere thickens. By 3 p.m. half the team is combing through email archives, the other half is rescanning notebooks for missing originals.

Manual compliance is like an old desktop computer that works fine until you open too many windows. Under audit load it hangs, buffers, and occasionally crashes.

4.1 The Psychological Cost

I have interviewed dozens of QA managers post-inspection. The common refrain: "We knew the data *existed*; we just couldn't *prove* it fast enough." That gap—between knowledge and demonstrability—is exactly where 483 observations are born.

5. A Case Study: The Day the Temperature Logs Betrayed Us

Let me share a real incident, anonymized for obvious reasons. A sterile manufacturing site relied on wall-mounted data loggers for cold room monitoring. Operators manually transferred the readings to a master spreadsheet at shift change, then printed and signed the sheet weekly. Sounds straightforward.

What went wrong?

- One logger's clock drifted by six hours after a daylight-saving change.
- The operator, seeing a "normal" reading, copied it without suspecting time misalignment.
- The deviation system was purely email-based. Nobody investigated the missing alert.
- During an MHRA inspection six months later, the auditor matched shipping batch numbers to the mis-timed logs. Every product shipped in a 14-day window fell under suspicion.

We spent nine months in remediation, including retrospective stability data, because a $50 wall clock battery died unnoticed. Manual compliance amplified a trivial hardware fault into a potential patient-safety crisis.

6. Traditional Fixes—and Why They Fail

Faced with incidents like the one above, companies usually reach for three standard remedies:

1. Add another SOP step.
2. Conduct refresher training.

3. Increase internal audit frequency.

These measures are not wrong; they're just insufficient.

6.1 SOPs: Band-Aids on Broken Processes

Adding steps rarely addresses root architectural flaws. You end up with 42-page SOPs nobody reads and that new hires cannot memorize. Complexity becomes a silent saboteur.

6.2 Training: The Leaky Bucket Phenomenon

People forget. Staff turnover is constant. Contract workers rotate. Training is vital but assuming it will eliminate routine data transfer errors is optimistic bordering on naïve.

6.3 Internal Audits: Looking Backward, Walking Forward

Internal audits often happen quarterly or annually. By the time findings emerge, the window for pro-active correction is gone. They reveal historical non-compliance but do not always prevent *current* errors from maturing into audit citations.

7. Where AI and Automation Can Help—But Only If Framed Correctly

Before we jump into solutions we need a disclaimer: AI is not a silver bullet. It does, however, excel at three things manual systems struggle with—scale, speed, and pattern recognition.

1. Scale
   Continuous monitoring of thousands of data points (temperatures, pressures, environmental particles) is trivial for machines, impossible for humans.

2. Speed
   Algorithms can surface anomalies in seconds, allowing interventions before deviations snowball.

3. Pattern Recognition
   Machine learning models can flag subtle shifts—like a gradual decline in equipment performance—that human reviewers miss because each day's data looks "normal" in isolation.

7.1 Real-Time Integrity Guards

Imagine a layer of automated checks that cross-verify time stamps, audit trails, and calibration status every time a value enters the system. The same battery failure in our cold-room story would trigger an instant, visible alert rather than a six-month forensic disaster.

7.2 Intelligent Documentation Workflows

Automation can pre-fill metadata, enforce mandatory fields, and prevent progression until critical controls are satisfied. That eliminates "blank boxes," missing initials, and wrong version templates—low-level errors that collectively erode inspector confidence.

7.3 Human-in-the-Loop Deviation Triage

Algorithms can classify deviations by risk level, suggest probable root causes based on historical patterns, and route high-risk cases for expedited SME review. People still decide; the system just shines a spotlight faster and brighter.

8. Common Pitfalls When Shifting from Manual to Automated Compliance

I have seen several automation projects fall into predictable traps. Avoiding them is half the battle.

- Garbage In, Garbage Out
  Feeding unvalidated historical data into a new AI model will propagate old errors at digital speed.

- Overtrust Syndrome
  Believing the system is "self-validating" leads to complacency. Remember: automation reduces manual workload, not accountability.
- Shadow Processes
  If unofficial spreadsheets or paper notes remain outside the automated ecosystem, data integrity gaps persist. Integration is non-negotiable.
- Change Fatigue
  Rolling out too many features at once overwhelms staff. Phased adoption aligned with user feedback mitigates resistance.

9. A Practical Framework: The Human-Machine Risk Lens

Here's a field-tested approach I recommend before any AI or automation initiative:

1. Map the Current State
   Document each step where humans create, modify, or transfer GMP data.
2. Classify Risk Points
   Rate each step by likelihood and impact of error during an audit scenario.
3. Assign Roles
   Decide where human judgment is irreplaceable and where machines can provide safeguarding redundancy.
4. Layer Controls
   For human-critical steps, add automated prompts or checks.

For machine-handled steps, establish human verification frequency.

5. Validate and Iterate
   Treat the framework itself as a living system. Schedule quarterly reviews to refine risk classes as operations evolve.

Think of it as dual-vision compliance: humans see context, machines watch patterns.

10. Key Takeaways

- Manual compliance systems were never designed for today's data volume, complexity, or regulatory scrutiny.
- Human cognitive limits make zero-defect manual data handling unrealistic.
- Compliance debt accumulates silently and crystallizes under audit pressure.
- Traditional fixes—more SOPs, more training, more audits—address symptoms, not root causes.
- AI and automation, properly framed, provide scalable, real-time safety nets without replacing human judgment.
- The Human-Machine Risk Lens helps teams transition from reactive, document-driven compliance to proactive, data-driven assurance.

Wrapping Up—and Setting the Stage

We have dissected why manual compliance is cracking under its own weight and how automation can, when used judiciously, bear some of that load. Yet I have warned repeatedly that AI is not a miracle cure. In the next chapter we will scrutinize that claim head-on. "AI Is Not Magic (And That's Why It Works)" will demystify algorithms, separate plausible benefits from science fiction, and give you the vocabulary to engage vendors, IT teams, and regulators with confidence. I'll meet you there.

Chapter 5

AI Is Not Magic (And That's Why It Works)

A Quick Breath Before We Dive In

In the last chapter we walked through the slow-motion car crash that happens when otherwise competent people depend on scattered spreadsheets, tribal knowledge, and heroic overtime to stay compliant. We saw why manual compliance, even when fueled by passion and caffeine, simply doesn't scale in a data-dense, globally networked, post-COVID supply chain. Now you and I need to switch gears.

If manual processes are fraying, does that mean we should hand the keys to a black-box algorithm and let it "handle compliance"? Absolutely not. In fact, that mindset is the surest way to trigger a 483.

This chapter is about building a sober, regulator-proof relationship with artificial intelligence. I am framing it deliberately as a relationship rather than a toolset. Magic is seductive; relationships are sometimes messy, but they are built on understanding. When you understand how AI really works—and, equally important, what it cannot do—you can deploy it like a reliable colleague rather than an exotic gadget.

1. Why "Magic" Thinking Creeps Into Pharma in the First Place

I still remember a pre-approval inspection where the plant manager—well respected, zero tolerance for nonsense—leaned toward the inspector and said, "We've implemented AI, so the system basically takes care of data integrity." You could have heard the collective exhale from QA. We were all thinking the same thing: *Please don't ask a follow-up question.*

The manager wasn't trying to deceive anyone; he was parroting a storyline sold to him by a slick vendor demo. Unfortunately, that storyline had three ingredients that show up in nearly every "AI is magic" pitch:

1. **Technological Awe** – The demo moves fast, dashboards shimmer, and colorful graphs animate in near real time.
2. **Oversimplified Cause–Effect** – "We trained the model on thousands of deviations, so it just knows."
3. **Displacement of Responsibility** – The insinuation that once the algorithm is deployed, humans can focus on "higher-value activities."

Each is tempting. Each feeds the daydream that compliance could become automatic, effortless, perhaps even invisible. And each erodes the very control mindset regulators look for.

2. How "Magic" Thinking Leads Straight to Audit Findings

Let me walk you through a composite scenario—drawn from pieces of real audits, blended to protect confidentiality—that shows how quickly magical thinking about AI can break down in front of an inspector.

The Set-Up

- A mid-sized European sterile injectables plant has adopted an AI-enabled monitoring platform for environmental data.
- The quality agreement states that any alert generated by the platform is automatically logged as an "Event" in the EQMS.
- The validation package focuses heavily on algorithm accuracy; it glosses over user governance.

The Audit

An EMA inspector asks a simple question: "When the algorithm throws an alert, who decides whether a formal deviation is required?"

Silence. Eventually a production supervisor says, "Well, the system flags anomalies, so we trust it. If there is no flag, we assume conditions are acceptable."

en minutes later the inspector finds a growth trend in viable particle counts that the algorithm did not classify as anomalous because it never breached the statistical threshold set during model training. The inspector's eyebrow goes up. Cue the 483 equivalent.

The Root Cause

The team unconsciously transferred the burden of trend recognition to the algorithm but failed to establish human oversight criteria. Because AI was perceived as magic, the governance guardrails that exist for any non-AI statistical quality control system were forgotten.

3. Why Traditional Corrective Actions Fall Short

You might think, "Easy fix—just tighten the algorithm's thresholds or add an SOP step." The problem is deeper. Traditional CAPAs tend to treat AI like conventional software:

- Update requirements specification.

- Revalidate the software release.
- Retrain staff on the new SOP.

Those steps are necessary but insufficient, because they do not address *concept drift* (the way underlying data patterns change over time) or *human drift* (how operators' trust in the system evolves). AI is dynamic; your compliance controls must be dynamic too, but deliberately so.

4. De-Mystifying AI: How It Really Works in Plain Language

If AI isn't magic, what is it? Let's strip away the jargon. Most AI you will meet in pharmaceutical operations falls into three functional families:

1. **Pattern Detectors** – Algorithms that recognize correlations in historical data and alert when the present stops looking like the past.
2. **Predictive Scorers** – Models that assign a probability to a future event, such as "likelihood this batch record requires an investigation."
3. **Natural Language Extractors** – Systems that sift through documents or free-text fields to pull out structured information, e.g., materials, deviation types, or change control rationale.

Notice what all three share: they process input, apply a learned statistical relationship, and deliver an output that can be summarized as a *probability* or *classification*. Nothing magical, nothing autonomous, just mathematics.

Even the most advanced deep-learning models are fundamentally sophisticated pattern matchers. They do not understand process criticality, regulatory context, or patient risk the way you and I do. They see numbers, not consequences.

5. Where AI Genuinely Excels—and Why That Matters in an Audit

Once we drop the magic narrative, we can appreciate AI for what it is spectacular at:

- **Speed** – Ingesting millions of rows of temperature, pressure, or micro counts every hour without fatigue.
- **Subtle Correlation** – Spotting weak signals that escape Shewhart charts or human review.
- **Consistency** – Applying the same statistical rules 24/7, immune to night-shift tiredness or weekend backlog.

In an audit setting, these strengths translate into a few tangible advantages:

- **Data Availability** – No scrambling for additional slicings of data; the model already stores segmentations for quick recall.
- **Evidence of Control** – If you can show real-time dashboards calibrated against validated acceptance criteria, you demonstrate proactive oversight.
- **Rapid Root-Cause Scoping** – When an inspector asks, "Have you seen this trend elsewhere?" an AI-driven query can surface correlating batches in seconds.

But—and this is crucial—these advantages only win credence when accompanied by transparent human governance.

6. Guardrails: A Practical Framework I Use With Clients

Over the past decade I've moved from AI enthusiast, to skeptic, to balanced practitioner. The framework I keep revisiting is simple enough to remember under audit stress yet robust enough to satisfy regulators:

1. **Define the Decision, Not the Algorithm.**
   Start by articulating the business or compliance decision: e.g., "Escalate to deviation when predicted contamination risk > 15%."

2. **Document Data Lineage.**
   For every data element the model ingests, map its origin (instrument, LIMS, MES), its transformation, and its owner.

3. **Validate for Fitness of Use, Not Perfection.**
   Aim to prove that the model performs *sufficiently* to support the decision. "Black-box explainability" cannot be an excuse for ignoring performance boundaries.

4. **Institute Human Check-Points.**
   At predetermined moments—alert generation, batch release review, trend report sign-off—a trained individual evaluates AI output against process knowledge.

5. **Monitor Model Drift Quarterly (Minimum).**
   Even stable processes change. Re-establish baselines periodically; archive snapshots of model parameters so you can demonstrate control over evolution.

6. **Escalate Discrepancies as Deviations, Not IT Tickets.**
   If AI suggests one action and human judgment suggests another, treat the gap as a potential quality event. This elevates governance from IT territory to QMS territory.

Clients who adopt these six guardrails rarely see AI-related observations. When observations do occur, they revolve around documentation gaps, not the algorithm's existence.

7. Common Pitfalls I Keep Seeing

Artificial intelligence might feel new, but the mistakes people make around it are strangely familiar. They echo classic GMP pitfalls:

- **Validation by Vendor Brochure** – Accepting marketing slides as evidence instead of performing user requirement specification and risk analysis.
- **Procedure-Less Deployment** – Piloting a model in production without updating the quality manual.
- **Outsourcing Accountability** – Assuming the data science team "owns" the outcome. Under GxP, the process owner owns the outcome, period.
- **Single-Point Dependency** – Designing the workflow so that if the algorithm is down, the process stalls. Inspectors abhor fragile systems.

Recognizing these anti-patterns early lets you embed preventive controls rather than scrambling for corrective ones.

8. A Day in the Life: How Realistic AI Fits a QA Professional's Routine

Let me narrate a typical morning for a QA associate—let's call her Priya—working in a biologics fill-finish facility that has embedded AI in its environmental and manufacturing data review.

1. **7:30 AM—Dashboard Digest**
   Priya reviews an overnight digest generated by the AI. It flags three batches with a 12–15% elevated risk of out-of-spec

endotoxin levels based on upstream bioreactor temperature micro-fluctuations.

2. **7:45 AM—Human Sanity Check**
   She pulls the original temperature trends, checks sensor calibration logs, and confirms the data are trustworthy.
3. **8:15 AM—Cross-Functional Huddle**
   Priya, manufacturing, and maintenance agree to increase sampling frequency for those batches. They treat the AI alert as a *signal*, not a verdict.
4. **9:00 AM—Documentation**
   She records the decision pathway in the QMS: data source, algorithm version, risk score, human rationale, action taken.
5. **10:30 AM—Audit Readiness**
   Priya files the AI digest into a "Continuous Verification" folder accessible to auditors. All transformations are traceable, including why the risk threshold is set at 10% and what evidence supports that limit.

No magic. Just a systematic, disciplined conversation between algorithm output and human judgment.

9. From Inspector Questions to Framework Answers

Below are real inspector questions I've encountered, followed by the framework-based answers that satisfied them.

Question: "How do you know the model is still valid nine months after deployment?"

Answer Framework: Present the quarterly drift analysis report, reference Procedure Q-AI-012, and show archival parameter snapshots proving less than 3% performance deviation.

Question: "If the model and operator disagree, who wins?"

Answer Framework: SOP Q-AI-004 mandates escalation to QA for arbitration. The divergence itself prompts a deviation workflow.

Question: "Who trained the algorithm?"

Answer Framework: Data scientists develop the model, but the process owner signs off on requirements and acceptance criteria. Documentation resides in the validation master plan annex.

10. The Mindset Shift You and I Must Embrace

Fundamentally, AI in pharma is about *probabilistic decision support* layered onto a deterministic regulatory environment. That tension requires a mindset shift from absolute to conditional thinking:

- Instead of "The batch is in or out of spec," think "The batch has a 7% projected risk of failure, warranting additional controls."
- Instead of "The algorithm is correct or incorrect," think "The algorithm adds a quantified perspective; I remain the decision owner."

When you internalize this mindset, AI becomes less a mystical oracle and more a new form of instrumentation—one that measures patterns. You wouldn't release product on a scale you never calibrated; likewise, you shouldn't rely on an algorithm you never validated.

11. Key Takeaways From This Chapter

- Magical thinking about AI sets the stage for audit findings by masking ownership and diminishing human oversight.
- AI's real strengths—speed, subtle correlation, consistency—are only valuable when harnessed through transparent guardrails.

- Governing AI requires additional layers beyond classic CSV: data lineage, model drift monitoring, and human-in-the-loop checkpoints.
- Pitfalls often mirror classic GMP weak spots: vendor over-reliance, procedure gaps, accountability diffusion, and fragile workflows.
- The winning mindset treats AI as probabilistic instrumentation, not autonomous authority.

12. Transitioning to the Next Chapter

Now that we've stripped away the illusion of AI as sorcery and replaced it with a grounded governance framework, we're ready to tackle a surprisingly thorny question: **How much automation is enough—and when does it cross the line into over-automation?** In the next chapter we'll dissect that boundary, exploring how to strike a balance that keeps your organization nimble without turning every task into a robot's job.

Chapter 6

Automation vs Over-Automation

A Brief Look Back

In the previous chapter I made a deliberate effort to demystify AI. We agreed that algorithms are neither pixie dust nor existential threat; they are, at best, disciplined assistants. But there is an uncomfortable corollary: once professionals finally grow comfortable with the idea of automating a task, they often swing too far in the other direction. I have watched well-intentioned quality leaders accumulate more bots, macros, and scheduled scripts than they have CAPAs, inadvertently creating a new kind of fragility.

Automation, used thoughtfully, can rescue you from audit chaos. Over-automation, used reflexively, can guarantee it. This chapter is about learning to tell the difference—and teaching your organization to do the same.

1. Why the Temptation to Automate Everything Exists

1.1 A Decade of Accumulated Pain

Walk through any pharmaceutical plant where electronic systems have gradually replaced paper and you will see layers: the original DCS, a 1990s LIMS, an early-2000s EDMS, add-on deviation trackers, and, recently, machine-learning dashboards. Each layer solved an urgent problem of its era but introduced new friction, and every audit re-exposes that friction. Understandably, the default reaction is, "Let's automate the friction away."

That impulse is not irrational. When a line operator spends forty minutes each shift re-entering batch numbers because two systems refuse to talk, automating the trans-entry feels like mercy. When a QA reviewer spends Friday night clicking through 287 log files looking for out-of-trend values, a Python script feels like liberation. We have experienced the pain of human-centric processes; therefore, the pendulum swings toward machine-centric ones.

1.2 Cultural Prestige: "Digital = Advanced"

There is also prestige attached to automation. Board presentations favor dashboards ablaze with real-time metrics; investors reward talk of "lights-out manufacturing." Nobody invites the head of quality to keynote a conference with a presentation titled "We decided not to automate." In that environment, restraint can look like stagnation and measured skepticism can be mistaken for Luddism.

1.3 The Fear of Human Error

Finally, there is a genuine and data-supported fear: people make mistakes. Data-integrity citations frequently reference manual transcription, manual calculations, or manual overrides. If an algorithm never types "0.3" when it means "0.03," why let a human near the keyboard at all? The assumption is that removing the human removes the error; therefore more automation must always be safer.

The assumption is comforting—until you remember who wrote the algorithm, configured the scheduler, and interpreted the output.

2. How Over-Automation Breeds New Audit Failures

To understand why inspectors raise eyebrows at "set-and-forget" systems, you must appreciate two audit realities:

- Inspectors distrust black boxes.
- Inspectors distrust broken boxes even more.

Let's examine how over-automation can create both.

2.1 Loss of Process Visibility

Imagine a deviation-tracking workflow that automatically assigns severity, selects the root-cause template, schedules preventive actions, and closes records after e-signatures. It sounds efficient—until an inspector asks, "Why was this repeat deviation categorized as minor?" If nobody in the room knows the classification logic baked into the script, you've replaced manual subjectivity with opaque subjectivity. The failure mode is now secrecy, not sloppiness.

2.2 Propagation of Hidden Logic Errors

When code autogenerates Certificate of Analysis statements, the very first mis-mapping of a specification triggers a cascade. The script never gets tired, never hesitates, and never self-corrects; it just multiplies the error across batches. I once observed a plant where automated label printing silently truncated the lot number during a string concatenation. The defect persisted for six months because "the system did it." By the time QA discovered it, 42 distribution lots were affected, all appropriately signed off inside the same "compliant" system.

2.3 Over-Reliance on System Availability

Over-automation also introduces a single-point-of-failure risk. If batch-record reviews depend on an NLP engine running on a single on-premises server, what happens when that server reboots mid-audit? I have seen inspectors flip through a stack of manually generated batch records while the IT group scrambles to restore a corrupted VM. The tension is palpable, and the narrative—"we can't function without our bot"—is devastating.

2.4 Complacency in Human Oversight

Perhaps the most insidious consequence is human deskilling. Once the system normalizes decision-making, operators may lose the habit of thinking. I once asked a line supervisor to walk me through the logic of an automated in-process control algorithm. His honest answer: "I don't know; it's in the SOP." That response is enough to trigger an inspector's reflexive suspicion: if you don't understand it, how do you know it is working today?

3. Traditional Mitigation Strategies—and Their Limits

Before we talk about using AI to avoid over-automation, let's look at what the industry already tries.

3.1 Validation by Exhaustive Testing

The conventional answer is "validate harder." We write thicker protocols, attempt 100 % test-case coverage, and file them in the DMS. But algorithms that change (or learn) over time defy exhaustive testing; a validation snapshot taken in January does not guarantee identical behavior in June. Moreover, the larger and more interconnected the automated estate, the more combinatorial the test matrix becomes. At some point the spreadsheet of test cases fractures under its own weight, and teams revert to partial coverage plus trust.

3.2 SOP Layers and "Human in the Loop" Sign-offs

Organizations add SOP steps requiring human review of automated outputs: "Step 5: Verify that the auto-calculated endotoxin limit equals ≤ 0.5 EU/mL." In principle this restores oversight; in practice the box gets ticked uncritically because the human trusts the system. The formality is preserved but the vigilance is not.

3.3 Periodic Re-qualification

Many sites schedule annual or bi-annual re-validation of automated workflows. This is not wrong, but it assumes that failures distribute conveniently around calendar anniversaries. If a labeling algorithm drifts four months after re-qualification, a six-month blind window remains—plenty of time for deviations to accumulate.

4. Where AI and Automation Genuinely Help—If You Apply Restraint

Here lies the paradox: the same AI capabilities that can over-automate you into opacity can, when deployed deliberately, balance the system and reduce risk. The governing principle is **selective augmentation**, not wholesale replacement.

Below I outline five design heuristics that separate useful automation from dangerous over-automation.

4.1 Make the Algorithm Explain Itself (Explainable AI)

At minimum, configure any classification or decision-making model to retain not only its output but also the key signals that informed that output. When an inspector asks why a process-simulation batch was flagged as "not representative," you can display the specific model weights or rule contributions: e.g., "The model weighted variation in mixing speed at 45 %, fill temperature at 30 %, and hold-time deviation at 25 %."

Explainability transforms a black box into a glass box. You still need human judgment, but the inspector sees a transparent chain of reasoning rather than a mystical decree.

4.2 Build Failsafe Degradation Paths

Every critical automated decision should have a pre-defined fallback that reverts to a simpler, auditable method. If the NLP-driven batch record summarizer encounters a corrupted file, the system should flag "manual review required" rather than improvise or remain silent. The fallback can be as mundane as emailing QA with a PDF attachment, but the principle is crucial: **never trap the business behind a locked algorithmic door**.

4.3 Layer, Don't Collapse, Decision Hierarchies

Use AI to surface anomalies and assemble evidence; let humans arbitrate. For example, an image-analysis engine can pre-screen visual inspection photos and rank potential defects. However, the final disposition should still require human confirmation. This layered approach keeps personnel cognitively engaged while focusing their attention on high-value inspections rather than on 100 % manual coverage.

4.4 Implement Living Validation (Continuous Verification)

Move from event-based validation to signal-based confidence. Instead of validating the algorithm once a year, continuously monitor performance indicators: false-positive rates, skipped-step alerts, and process drift metrics. When any indicator exceeds a pre-defined threshold, the system automatically triggers a micro-re-qualification step or human review. Continuous verification acknowledges that algorithms evolve and that validation must evolve with them.

4.5 Preserve Skill Redundancy in People

Design SOPs that rotate personnel through manual versions of key tasks at defined intervals—think of airline pilots practicing manual landings. If an anomaly suddenly disables the automated sterile-filtration scheduler, at least one engineer on every shift should remember how to reconstruct the sequence manually. Far from undermining automation, this human resilience reassures inspectors that the plant can think for itself.

5. Common Mistakes When Pursuing "Lights-Out" Quality

Even seasoned teams stumble into the same traps. Recognize them early, and you can redirect before the CAPA backlog testifies against you.

1. Automating an unclear process
   If you can't articulate the logic on paper, encoding it in Python multiplies confusion. Automation should clarify ambiguity, not enshrine it.
2. Confusing speed with control
   Faster deviation closure is meaningless if root-cause analysis deteriorates. Inspectors sense when the timeline looks too tidy to be true.
3. Neglecting data provenance
   ETL (Extract-Transform-Load) pipelines often reshape data silently. Without lineage tracking, you cannot prove that the 0.12 µg/L impurity result originated from the instrument you think it did
4. Ignoring the audit trail of the automation itself
   Many custom scripts log the user who executed them (often a

service account) but omit configuration versioning. Auditors will ask: "Which model version generated this prediction?"

5. Treating configuration as code and calling it "validated"—then letting it drift
   If a configuration change can alter behavior, you must control that change. A CSV file of parameters sitting in someone's downloads folder is not an audit-ready configuration.
6. Allowing IT to own GxP responsibilities by default
   Technical ownership does not equal quality ownership. The moment quality disengages from automated workflows, a compliance vacuum forms.

6. A Practical Framework: The Automation Balance Canvas

During consulting workshops I use a one-page template called the Automation Balance Canvas. You can replicate it on a whiteboard or in a simple spreadsheet. The objective is to reach a balanced automation strategy for any given process.

1. Process Step
   • Describe the current manual or semi-manual step.
2. Risk if Manual
   • Rate on a scale of 1–5 the probability of error and its impact.
3. Benefit if Automated
   • Estimate time saved, error reduction, or data-integrity improvement.
4. Risk if Over-Automated
   • Consider loss of visibility, deskilling, single-point-of-failure risk.

5. Explainability Requirement
   • Define what evidence must be available for each automated decision.
6. Fallback Strategy
   • Document the reversion plan and the trigger criteria.
7. Validation & Monitoring Plan
   • Identify metrics that form the living validation loop.
8. Human Skill Retention Plan
   • Specify training or rotation to keep people competent.

Teams fill the canvas line-by-line for every critical operation—environmental monitoring trending, cleaning-validation scheduling, batch-record compilation, and so on. The result is a map of where automation should act as "muscle" and where humans must remain "brain." Inspectors love seeing this kind of structured thinking; it demonstrates conscious risk management rather than technology fascination.

7. Illustrative Scenario: Filling Line Out-of-Spec Alerts

To bring these abstractions to life, let's walk through a composite scenario loosely based on observations from multiple sites.

7.1 The Legacy Situation

Operators on a high-speed vial filling line manually watch pressure readings on an HMI. If differential pressure across the HEPA filter drops below set-point, they must pause the line, perform an integrity check, and document the action. Inevitably, operators sometimes miss the moment the needle dips, or they spot it but decide it is transient. During a 2021 inspection, the facility received an observation: "Failure to maintain aseptic assurance due to delayed reaction to differential-pressure excursions."

7.2 The First Automation Attempt

The engineering group installs a script that polls the PLC every second, logs pressure, and auto-emails alerts to QA if pressure breaches set-points for more than 10 seconds. Operators still sign batch records manually; the system merely accelerates notification. Initially, inspectors praise the proactivity.

7.3 The Over-Automation Creep

Six months later, a second script automatically pauses the line and annotates the batch record if the alert triggers. A third script auto-generates a deviation in the quality system, assigns severity "Major," and proposes root cause "HVAC performance." Operators gradually disengage; they wait for the email to tell them what to do.

During a subsequent audit, the inspector asks, "Why was this excursion classified as Major rather than Critical? What algorithmic logic made that determination?" The site cannot answer: the logic is embedded in version 3.7 of a script whose author left the company. The observation reads: "Lack of documented rationale for severity classification algorithm. Inadequate assurance that safety impact properly evaluated."

7.4 Rescuing the Situation with Balanced Automation

The site walks through the Automation Balance Canvas:

- Risk if Manual: high (missed excursions)
- Benefit if Automated: immediate alerting, objective logging
- Risk if Over-Automated: mis-classification, lack of human judgment

They decide to retain automatic alerts and automatic line pause (with a manual override under controlled procedure) but remove automatic severity assignment. The script now populates proposed severity and evidence, but QA must confirm or edit before the deviation locks. Additionally, the algorithm logs its variable weights, and the configuration file sits under version control inside the validated environment. Continuous monitoring compares algorithm suggestions with human overrides to detect drift.

During the next audit, inspectors see transparency, a clear fallback path, and active human oversight. No observations.

8. The Human Dimension: Teaching "Judicious Laziness"

One fear managers express is that partial automation feels like an admission of defeat—or, worse, creates inefficiency by making people re-do what the system already did. I prefer the aviation analogy: auto-pilots fly most of the cruise phase, but pilots remain mentally alert. They practice "judicious laziness": letting the machine handle the repetitive while preserving capacity for the unexpected.

To cultivate this in pharma, training must evolve. Instead of teaching operators to follow 47 clicks in a deviation-closure wizard, teach them to interpret anomalies the wizard flags. Instead of rushing to retire senior analysts because "the software can trend stability faster," keep them as mentors who can spot an implausible trend and say, "Wait, that looks like a calibration artifact."

Judicious laziness is not a luxury; it is a defense against the brittleness of over-automation.

9. Regulatory Perspectives on Automation Scope

Regulators do not oppose automation. Annex 11, 21 CFR Part 11, and PIC/S PI 011 all encourage computerized systems—provided they are validated, controlled, and transparent. Guidance documents increasingly reference machine learning under the same umbrella of risk-based thinking.

However, when inspectors encounter a system that absolves humans of accountability, they tighten the screws. They ask for:

- Evidence the algorithm was fit for purpose
- Documentation that subject-matter experts reviewed and accepted its logic
- Demonstration that outputs are monitored for performance drift
- Confirmation that unusual outputs trigger human review

Failing to satisfy these items leads to citations that hurt not only the plant but also individual careers. Understanding how far is too far is therefore not academic; it is professional self-preservation.

10. Key Takeaways

1. Automation solves real pain but can introduce opaque risks.
2. Over-automation fails audits when logic becomes invisible, errors propagate silently, or human vigilance erodes.
3. Traditional mitigation (more testing, more SOPs) helps but cannot fully address evolving algorithms.
4. The remedy is selective augmentation: explainable AI, layered decision hierarchies, continuous verification, and preserved human skills.

5. Use frameworks like the Automation Balance Canvas to quantify benefits, risks, and fallback strategies.
6. Train people in "judicious laziness"—letting algorithms do the rote work without abdicating judgment.
7. Regulators support automation when it remains transparent, validated, and under human control.

Master the balance, and automation becomes a safety net rather than a trip wire.

Transition to Part 3

Now that we understand the fine line between empowering automation and over-engineering ourselves into vulnerability, we can focus on daily practices that keep plants eternally inspection-ready. In Part 3, we shift from philosophy to execution: applying AI for audit survival—not once a year, but continuously.

Chapter 7

AI-Powered Audit Readiness (Daily, Not Event-Based)

Setting the Scene—Why "Audit Readiness" Is Usually an Illusion

Walk into almost any pharmaceutical plant three weeks before a scheduled regulatory inspection and you will feel the temperature rise—not in the granulation suite, but in the war rooms where binders, spreadsheets, and nerves pile up simultaneously. "Audit readiness" becomes the only phrase anyone can utter. You know the ritual: night shifts dedicated to document reconciliation, frantic e-mails to vendors for missing calibration certificates, risk assessments rewritten on the fly, and a sudden spike in "updated" SOPs that look suspiciously similar to last year's.

Yet for all the late-night heroics, many companies still receive Form 483s or critical deficiencies. How does that happen when teams "worked so hard" before the audit? The unpleasant answer is that audit readiness was treated as an **event** rather than a **continuous operational state**. In this chapter we will replace the adrenaline-driven scramble with an AI-supported, quietly confident routine—one that happens every day, often imperceptibly, so that the inspection becomes just another Tuesday.

1. Why the Fire-Drill Model of Audit Preparation Persists

1.1 Legacy of Paper and Periodic Review

Historically, data sat in logbooks, binders, local servers, and even personal hard drives. Retrieval was manual, so the natural—even rational—response was to batch documentation work into periodic reviews: annual product quality reviews (APQRs), biennial equipment qualification, and so on. Over time the habit hardened into culture: "We'll get everything in order before the auditors arrive."

1.2 The Comfort of the Known Deadline

A scheduled FDA pre-approval inspection or an announced MHRA surveillance visit gives teams a concrete date. Human psychology loves a countdown; managers can schedule resources against it. Unannounced or for-cause inspections are rarer, so the illusion that preparedness can be time-boxed survives, even though regulators explicitly state that compliance must be maintained at every moment.

1.3 KPI Theater Over Process Integrity

Many sites measure audit readiness by superficial metrics: percentage of SOPs within review cycle, number of open CAPAs, or training completion rates. These can be gamed—documents updated without substantive change, CAPAs closed "administratively," training signed off before competence is demonstrated. On paper the site looks fine; in practice, latent risk accumulates.

2. How Event-Based Readiness Fails During Real Audits

1. Data Silos Get Exposed

Inspectors increasingly use data-driven sampling—asking for raw electronic records, cross-referencing batch manufacturing,

QC results, and warehouse transactions. If those datasets live in different systems, reconciliation errors surface instantly.

2. Human Memory Bottlenecks

During an inspection, the person who "fixed" a deviation narrative the night before might be at lunch when the inspector asks about it. The paper tells one story; the individual recollection tells another. Discrepancies create distrust.

3. Stress Reveals Gaps

Over-coached staff may recite prepared answers that collapse under follow-up questions. When floor operators nervously flip through logbooks, any missing entry, correction without reason, or unexplained timestamp looks like data fabrication.

4. Quality Culture Appears Cosmetic

Inspectors sense when compliance is cosmetic. They will probe deeper, and small inconsistencies cascade into systemic observations—"If you missed this, what else have you missed?" That's how a minor lapse transforms into multi-page 483s.

3. The Continuous Readiness Philosophy

Continuous readiness is not about racing faster; it is about **making the race disappear**. When every compliance obligation—documentation, review, deviation handling, calibration, preventive maintenance—flows as an ordinary workstream, the site is inspection-ready by default. The operator signs contemporaneously because it is easier than back-dating. The analyst completes metadata because the system won't accept partial entries. The quality reviewer focuses on anomalies, not on hunting paper.

But habitual readiness has two prerequisites:

- **Visibility**—knowing automatically, at any moment, whether each GxP element is in a state of control.
- **Feedback**—detecting drift early enough to intervene with minimal disruption.

Both needs are perfectly matched to AI and automation capabilities. The role of AI here is not to "pass the audit for you," but to act as a real-time sensor network for your compliance health.

4. Where Traditional Approaches Fall Short

4.1 Manual Dashboards Lag Reality

Even well-designed Excel trackers represent yesterday's data at best. Someone must pull entries from multiple systems, reconcile them, and update metrics. By the time the dashboard shows "overdue training," the employee might already be working unsupervised on a critical batch.

4.2 SOPs Cannot Anticipate Micro-Variations

Procedures describe typical flows, but in practice every deviation, skip-step, or instrument hiccup creates nuance. Human supervisors can't monitor thousands of micro-events daily; they rely on staff to report exceptions. Under time pressure, exceptions get rationalized away.

4.3 Periodic Reviews Hide Trend Signals

Annual or quarterly reviews summarize deviations, OOS, environmental excursions. But emerging signals—say, a subtle rise in micro counts in a specific clean room—may be lost in averages. Problems then erupt just before an audit, forcing retrospective justifications.

4.4 Cultural Fatigue

Continuous manual monitoring demands relentless vigilance. People eventually prioritize production quotas or personal convenience. Without supportive technology, sustainable daily readiness becomes an exhausting ideal.

5. What "AI-Powered" Really Means in Daily Practice

Before diving into concrete examples, let me clarify what we will and will not claim:

- We are **not** talking about black-box algorithms overwriting SOPs.
- We are **not** delegating final QA responsibility to software.
- We are **definitely** talking about augmenting human senses—surfacing weak signals, automating tedious cross-checks, and documenting evidence chains in real time.

Think of AI here as an omnipresent junior auditor who never sleeps, highlights risk as it emerges, and supplies you with tidy evidence packets for every decision.

6. Core Capabilities of AI-Powered Readiness

6.1 Contextual Data Stitching

Pharma data live in heterogenous environments: batch records, LIMS, EMS, ERP, MES, QMS. AI-driven middleware can align these streams by timestamp, equipment ID, batch number, analyst, material lot, and even environmental location. Instead of you comparing a microbiology alert in LIMS to HVAC pressure logs, the system correlates them and flags an exposure scenario instantly.

6.2 Pattern Recognition and Drift Detection

Machine-learning models can learn the "shape" of routine operations—temperature profiles of sterilization cycles, analyst signature patterns, environmental trends. When a new record deviates beyond natural variation, you receive an alert before it grows into a deviation. Crucially, the model must explain *why* the record looks different, providing interpretable features (for example: "Cycle F0 value 12% lower than historical median for load type C"). Regulators increasingly expect this level of transparency.

6.3 Natural-Language Document Understanding

Quality systems are flooded with text: SOPs, batch narratives, deviation reports, cleaning records. AI-based language models can pre-screen for missing impact assessment, inconsistent root cause logic, or non-GxP language ("accidentally," "probably," "maybe"). They do not replace human reviewers; they simply point to places your eyes should linger.

6.4 Predictive Capacity/Bottleneck Forecasting

By learning queues in maintenance, calibration, or CAPA closure workflows, AI can forecast when you'll cross regulatory time limits. Instead of discovering on day 30 that an investigation remains open, the system nudges responsible parties well in advance—"CAPA 22-104 is trending late; at current comment-resolution velocity it will breach the 30-day window."

6.5 Evidence Chain Automation

Every flagged anomaly can be attached automatically with raw data extracts, audit trails, and investigator comments. What took hours of gathering during audit prep happens contemporaneously, preserving metadata integrity and reducing reliance on memory.

7. Daily Workflow—A Walk-Through Example

Let's accompany a hypothetical QC analyst, Parul, and the QA reviewer, Miguel, through a routine day enhanced by AI-powered readiness.

1. Morning System Health Snapshot
At 8:00 a.m. Miguel opens his Quality Operations Dashboard. Overnight, the AI stitched together logs from the environmental monitoring system, trending microbiology results, and MES batch statuses. A heat map shows all production suites green except Room 3A, which turned amber because two viable particle counts edged near alert level. The AI correlates this with an HVAC filter nearly due for replacement. Miguel schedules maintenance before the day's fill starts—problem averted, evidence captured.

2. Real-Time Batch Execution
Parul starts executing a dissolution test in LIMS. The system pre-fills method parameters and checks calibration status of the apparatus. When Parul tries to load the sample earlier than the prescribed equilibration time, the software blocks the action and displays the relevant SOP excerpt. No need for a deviation write-up later.

3. Contextual Document Review
Later, Miguel reviews a deviation report drafted by another colleague. The AI reviewer highlights a sentence: "The root cause is likely operator distraction." It flags the phrase "likely" as non-deterministic and suggests checking training records and shift logs. Miguel digs deeper, finds the operator had a 12-hour shift against policy, and updates the root cause accordingly. The inspection trail now contains the AI prompt, Miguel's notes, and supporting timeclock data.

4. End-of-Day Readiness Score

Before leaving, Miguel checks the site readiness index—an amalgamation of open-item risk scores, critical equipment state, and deviation backlog. It reads 92/100. Anything below 90 triggers a management escalation. Everyone sleeps easier.

Notice what did **not** happen: all-hands war rooms, rushed document edits, or awkward "find that temperature chart" hunts. Readiness emerged as a by-product of normal work, guided by AI.

8. Architecting the System Without Over-Engineering

Automation does not mean building a monolithic platform. Most plants already have multiple validated systems. The goal is to create a **decision layer** that sits above them, draws context, and delivers insights. Key architectural principles:

- **Interoperability First**—use open data standards (where available) or validated connectors.
- **Explainability Built-In**—every alert must link back to raw data and a human-readable rationale.
- **Minimal Intrusion**—systems should guide, not disrupt. Hard stops only where absolutely necessary (e.g., calibration expired).
- **Scalable Granularity**—start with a subset of critical processes (sterile fill, OOS review) and expand gradually.

9. Governance and Human Oversight

AI can surface, rank, and even draft actions, but the QA unit retains final authority. Best practice governance includes:

- A **cross-functional AI steering committee**—QA, QC, IT, and operations jointly approve model releases.
- **Change control integration**—any model parameter shift follows formal change control with impact assessment.
- **Periodic model performance review**—accuracy metrics, false positives/negatives, and bias checks documented every quarter.
- **Inspector transparency protocol**—a concise document explaining algorithm scope, validation evidence, and user controls, ready to provide during audits.

10. Common Mistakes to Avoid

1. Treating AI like Another Point Solution

Bolting on a flashy anomaly-detection tool without system context leads to alert fatigue and distrust. Connect the dots first, then deploy intelligence.

2. Ignoring User Experience

If alerts arrive in a separate portal nobody checks, they are useless. Deliver insights in existing workflows—e-mail, MES interface, or mobile app depending on role.

3. Over-Automating Signatures

Electronic signatures must remain deliberate. Auto-clicking or default sign-offs erode the very data integrity you aim to strengthen.

4. Underestimating Validation Effort

Even though most AI logic sits in a decision layer, its outputs influence GMP decisions. IQ/OQ/PQ principles still apply, adapted for adaptive algorithms.

5. Targeting Perfection on Day One

Start with high-impact, well-bounded use cases: environmental trend detection or CAPA cycle-time prediction. Demonstrate value, then iterate.

11. A Practical Framework—The Five-Layer Model of Daily AI Readiness

1. Data Foundation

Clean, contemporaneous data entry; validated interfaces; audit trails intact.

2. Aggregation Layer

Secure pipelines bring disparate data into a unified lake or mesh with time-series context.

3. Intelligence Layer

ML models, rule engines, and NLP algorithms analyze aggregated data, producing interpretable signals.

4. Action Layer

Alerts routed to the right roles, SOP-linked guidance, and automated evidence packaging.

5. Governance Layer

Change control, periodic reviews, and regulatory transparency.

Visualize these layers as concentric circles. Weakness in the foundation propagates outward; robustness amplifies insights.

12. Cultivating the Right Mindset

Remember, the goal is not to impress inspectors with flashy dashboards. It is to create a workplace where compliance is a side effect of doing the job properly. AI enables that, but only if you:

- View alerts as **conversation starters**, not orders.

- Encourage staff to challenge or refine AI suggestions; that dialogue improves models and fosters ownership.
- Celebrate near-miss detection as a win, not a blame opportunity. Every alert resolved upstream of an audit protects the organization and the individual's reputation.

13. Case Study—Turning a Crisis Into Continuous Readiness

Three years ago, a mid-size sterile injectables plant in the Midwest received six FDA 483 observations, four related to data integrity. The QA head, Anita, almost resigned. Instead, she spearheaded a phased AI-readiness program:

Phase 1—Data Consolidation
MES, LIMS, and EMS logs were synchronized nightly. No predictive models yet—just visibility.

Phase 2—Anomaly Detection on Environmental Data
Within two months, the AI flagged intermittent spikes in non-viable particle counts. Investigation traced it to cleaning schedule overlap with HVAC damper cycling—an easy fix.

Phase 3—NLP Review of Deviation Reports
The system highlighted logical gaps in impact assessments, reducing supplemental information requests by 70%.

Outcome
During the next FDA surveillance audit, inspectors noted the proactive monitoring system and issued zero observations on data integrity. Staff reported a 40% reduction in overtime before the audit. Anita kept her job, but more importantly, she restored confidence across the plant.

14. Key Takeaways

- Event-based "panic prep" is a legacy of paper systems; it fails under modern data scrutiny.
- Continuous readiness requires two pillars: real-time visibility and timely feedback—areas where AI excels as a supportive layer.
- Successful deployment hinges on interoperable architecture, explainability, and tight governance.
- Start small, focus on high-risk processes, and integrate insights into everyday workflows.
- The ultimate metric is psychological: when audits feel routine rather than existential, your AI readiness program is working.

Transition to Next Chapter

Now that we have established how AI keeps you calmly inspection-ready every day, it is time to tackle one of the most dreaded—and common—sources of regulatory pain: data integrity breaches. In the next chapter we will move from general readiness to the specific mechanisms by which AI can **prevent data integrity failures before they happen**, safeguarding both your license to operate and your professional credibility.

Chapter 8

Preventing Data Integrity Failures Before They Happen

A Natural Next Step

In the previous chapter we moved the discussion from "audits as a panic event" to "audit readiness as a daily discipline." You saw how AI-driven vigilance can surface weak signals long before an inspector arrives. Now we zoom in on the single topic that still keeps seasoned professionals awake the night before any inspection: data integrity.

If compliance were a fortress, data integrity would be its foundation stones—once they crack, everything above collapses. Every major regulatory action of the last decade—483s, Warning Letters, import alerts, consent decrees—lists data integrity breaches as a root cause. By the time failure becomes visible, it is often too late. People lose credibility and sometimes their careers.

In this chapter I want to do something audacious yet entirely practical: reframe data integrity from a forensic after-the-fact exercise to a proactive, real-time discipline that is fully compatible with GxP and rooted in the ordinary work you already do. We will explore how considered use of AI and automation can make that shift possible without drowning you in new complexity or vendor-driven hype.

1. Why Data Integrity Keeps Slipping Through the Cracks

1.1 The Myth of "One Bad Actor"

When a breach surfaces, the narrative often focuses on a single analyst who allegedly deleted files or rewrote chromatography sequences. Inspectors know better. Systemic pressures—production targets, staffing shortages, chaotic document flows—nudge well-meaning people toward risky shortcuts. The "bad actor" story is convenient but incomplete, and it blinds organizations to the patterns that enable failure.

1.2 Hidden Complexity in Modern Workflows

Consider a single batch record today:

- An MES captures in-process parameters.
- LIMS stores analytical results and merges metadata.
- The DMS holds scanned logbooks from an auxiliary reactor still on paper.
- An ERP syncs material genealogy overnight.

Each handoff is an opportunity for data drift, time-stamp discrepancies, or silent overwrites. Yet SOPs usually describe tasks in isolated silos. The lived cross-system complexity is invisible until an inspector triangulates logs on Day 3 of an audit and the story no longer adds up.

1.3 The Cost of Retrospective Review

Traditional data integrity programs rely on periodic review: a QA associate prints an audit-trail, high-lights unusual events, and files a summary report. It feels thorough, but it is fundamentally backward-looking. At best, it limits the regulatory damage once a deviation has already occurred. At worst, it produces a false sense of security because the reviewer cannot possibly eyeball every entry in multi-gigabyte logs.

1.4 Cognitive Overload

Paper or digital, humans can process only so many variables simultaneously. When a chromatographer juggles pressure variations, sample queues, and device calibrations, they seldom notice a metadata mismatch or a subtle audit-trail gap. Data integrity breaches rarely look like smoking guns in real time; they are tiny discrepancies that coalesce into a pattern only in hindsight.

2. How Data Integrity Failures Trigger Audit Disasters

1. Snowball Effect: A single unexplained "deleted result" in a CDS can lead an inspector to expand the sample set. One finding multiplies into many.
2. Credibility Erosion: Once trust erodes, inspectors apply heightened scrutiny. Even compliant areas begin to look suspect.
3. Cascade into Systems-Level Citations: Data integrity is not an isolated item in 21 CFR 211 or EU GMP Annex 11. It links to validation, training, SOP adequacy, and management oversight. One local breach can convert into a systemic citation.
4. Career Collateral Damage: Individuals associated—sometimes tangentially—with a breach may face job stagnation, personal liability under certain jurisdictions, or visa issues if they are expatriates.

3. Why Classical Controls Stall

3.1 SOP Inflation

The knee-jerk response to any breach is another SOP. Over time you end up with a labyrinth of procedures that frontline staff neither read nor fully understand. Volume masquerades as rigor.

3.2 Periodic Audits as Silver Bullets

Annual internal audits are valuable, but the attack surface of data systems changes daily: new software patches, ad-hoc macros, hidden Excel formulas. Waiting six or twelve months to examine logs is akin to checking tire pressure after the car skids off the road.

3.3 Human Double-Checking Bias

Having a second person sign off does not neutralize human blind spots; it duplicates them. If the first reviewer misses a tampered time-stamp, the second reviewer tends to inherit the same assumption chain.

3.4 Reactive Forensics

Most forensic tools illuminate what went wrong after an incident. Root-cause analysis may satisfy regulatory closure requirements, but it seldom prevents recurrence in a fast-evolving environment.

4. Where AI and Automation Provide Real, Regulator-Friendly Help

AI, in the context we care about, is not a magic wand. Think of it instead as assisted pattern recognition and relentless timing discipline. It shines in three domains:

Speed: Machines parse gigabytes of audit-trail data in minutes, not days.

Anomaly Focus: Algorithms flag outliers for human judgment, preserving human expertise for decisions rather than hunting for needles in haystacks.

Context Linking: By correlating metadata across systems, AI reveals gaps that no single system view exposes.

Let's unpack each domain with concrete scenarios.

4.1 Real-Time Audit-Trail Surveillance

Imagine chromatography systems where audit-trail events stream into a monitoring layer. The algorithm learns routine patterns—sample runs, pauses for column conditioning, calibration injections—and flags deviations like an unexpected sequence abort followed by data deletion. The analyst receives a prompt minutes later, while memory of what actually happened is still fresh enough for accurate deviation entry. The same alert also routes to QA, creating transparency without manual data pulls.

4.2 Metadata Concordance Checks

When MES records a parameter at 13:45 h and LIMS receives the corresponding analytical result stamped 13:10 h, a 35-minute negative time gap appears. Individually, both systems think they are correct—the error surfaces only in the integration layer. AI models tuned to acceptable deviation windows can surface such mismatches, prompting immediate reconciliation before they grow into narrative inconsistencies.

4.3 Intelligent "Audit-Trail of the Audit-Trail"

Beyond monitoring first-order events, automation can verify the integrity of the logging mechanism itself—e.g., sudden gaps in entry density or suspiciously synchronized user logins that exceed human reaction times. This meta-layer aligns with the regulators' own forensic methods.

4.4 Human-Centered Design

The goal is not to replace human reviewers but to change their role from exhaustive record scanning to informed decision-making. The system says: "Here are the three events you actually need to look at," rather than dumping 15,000 lines of raw logs. Human expertise is preserved, cognition is respected, and fatigue risk declines.

5. Common Pitfalls When Introducing AI-Driven Monitoring

1. Data Swamp Creation: Capturing audit-trail streams without curation leads to unwieldy storage and no insight. Apply retention rules and indexing from day one.
2. Black-Box Anxiety: If end users cannot see why an alert appeared, they will mistrust it. Provide explain-ability—simple English explanations, not just probability scores.
3. Over-Alerting: Too many false positives push people back to ignoring the system. Calibrate thresholds iteratively with QA and operations feedback.
4. Ignoring Change Control: An algorithm's model version is itself GxP-relevant. Treat model updates like software patches—document, test, approve.
5. Assuming Universal Applicability: A model trained on one site's workflow may misinterpret another site's processes. Local contextualization is mandatory.

6. A Pragmatic Framework: The ADEPT Model

To keep preventive data integrity actionable I use the mnemonic ADEPT—Anticipate, Detect, Evaluate, Prevent, Track. Each stage maps to concrete steps, many of which can be augmented by AI.

6.1 Anticipate

Map critical data paths from generation to archival. Identify potential failure modes: manual transcriptions, system interfaces, time-zone conversions. Automation helps by creating real-time data lineage diagrams that update when configurations change.

6.2 Detect

Deploy continuous surveillance at handoff points. Machine-learning anomaly modules flag timestamp gaps, record edits, and unusual user behaviors.

6.3 Evaluate

Human experts receive prioritized alerts. A cross-functional triage (QA, IT, operations) assesses legitimacy within defined timelines (e.g., 24 h for high-risk events). The evaluation step retains human ethical and regulatory judgment.

6.4 Prevent

Use insights to refine processes—simple UI changes, added scanner validation at logbook digitization, or revised training. A feedback loop configures the detection threshold dynamically.

6.5 Track

Embed metrics into management review: number of critical alerts, mean time to evaluation, recurrence rate of specific event types. These KPIs demonstrate ongoing control to inspectors and senior management alike.

7. Implementation Roadmap Without Vendor Hype

1. Baseline Assessment: Inventory existing audit-trail sources, storage formats, and accessibility.

2. Governance Charter: Define roles—data owner, algorithm owner, QA oversight, IT custodian.
3. Pilot Scope: Choose one high-risk system (e.g., HPLC CDS) and one cross-platform interface (MES-LIMS). Avoid boiling the ocean.
4. Data Pipeline Hardening: Secure and version-control ETL scripts even if they are simple SQL queries; they are part of the validated state.
5. Algorithm Selection: Use transparent statistical models first (control charts, rule-based flags) before graduating to neural nets. Simpler models are easier to validate and explain.
6. Validation Strategy: Treat the monitoring layer as category 4 software under GAMP 5 (configurable) unless custom code pushes it to category 5. Document test scripts for normal and outlier datasets.
7. Training & Change Management: Conduct scenario-based training—show real alerts, not generic slides. Capture user feedback for threshold tuning.
8. Scale-Out Plan: After successful pilot metrics (reduced uninvestigated events by X %, audit-trail review time down by Y %), expand in concentric circles to other labs and manufacturing lines.
9. Continuous Improvement: Schedule quarterly model performance reviews; decommission metrics that no longer add value.

8. Case Study—Catching the Invisible Injection Peak

Background

A sterile injectables plant uses seven identical HPLC systems. During a mock pre-approval inspection, corporate QA noticed multiple "Delete Result" events across three systems. The site argued these were legitimate blank runs removed after confirmation. The phrase "Delete Result" alone alarmed management. They asked for a preventive solution, not another SOP.

Automated Intervention

A modest rules-engine was installed to stream every audit-trail line to a secure analytical buffer. Two weeks later the system flagged a pattern: certain analysts performed a "Run Stop" followed by "Delete Result" within a 90-second window, always between 17:45 and 18:00 h.

Human Evaluation

The QA reviewer learned that analysts were stopping runs to leave on time for the evening shuttle, deleting partial injections to avoid extended baselines. The practice, while culturally understandable, violated ALCOA+ principles.

Outcome

Management revised shift schedules and introduced auto-sampler queues that finish before handover. The monitoring threshold for run-stop events was calibrated to allow genuine instrument errors but still capture early terminations.

Result

In the next internal audit cycle, "Delete Result" events dropped by 93 %, and the site entered the FDA inspection anecdotally "boring"—no data integrity findings. The AI layer didn't punish staff; it revealed pressure points so the organization could adapt.

9. Human Factors Still Matter—Bridging Technology and Culture

1. Psychological Safety
   People must believe alerts are for support, not surveillance witch hunts. Invite end users to co-design dashboards, which increases trust and quality of feedback.
2. Narrative Framing
   Explain that inspectors already have comparable forensic tools. Choosing ignorance is not a shield; proactive monitoring is a career life-jacket.
3. Skill Elevation
   When manual log scanning disappears, freed-up time should be reinvested in analytical thinking—root-cause analysis, method development, continuous improvement. Automation becomes an enabler of professional growth, not role erosion.

10. Regulatory Alignment Check

- 21 CFR 11.10(e) requires "secure, computer-generated, time-stamped audit trails." Continuous AI-based review strengthens, not replaces, that requirement.
- EU GMP Annex 11, clause 9—"Audit trails need to be available and convertible to a generally intelligible form." Dashboards can export raw trails and annotated alerts to PDF/CSV for inspector review.
- MHRA "GXP Data Integrity Guidance," section 9.7, encourages "automation of exception reports." Our approach ticks that exact box.

We remain fully within the regulatory spirit: humans remain final decision-makers; systems merely surface exceptions faster.

11. Key Takeaways

- Data integrity breaches rarely start with a villain; they grow from systemic blind spots.
- Traditional retrospective reviews are too slow and too narrow for today's data volumes and cross-system complexity.
- AI's primary value lies in tireless pattern recognition and anomaly flagging, not in autonomous decision-making.
- Implement a staged ADEPT framework—Anticipate, Detect, Evaluate, Prevent, Track—to embed prevention in daily operations.
- Treat AI models and their updates as GxP-relevant assets subject to change control and validation.
- Human factors—trust, training, cultural pressures—must be addressed alongside technology to achieve sustainable integrity.
- Done right, proactive data integrity monitoring turns inspections from high-stakes detective stories into routine confirmation exercises, protecting both the organization and individual careers.

A Glance Forward

Now that we've explored how AI can inoculate your data against silent corruption, the logical question is: what about documents—the narrative layer that ties data together? In the next chapter we'll shift focus to smart document review and how automation reduces the inevitable human blind spots that creep into batch records, protocols, and SOPs.

Chapter 9

Smart Document Review & Reducing Human Blind Spots

Lead-In from the Previous Chapter

In the last chapter we wrestled with data integrity and the silent ways bits and bytes betray us during inspections. Now we turn to the medium that still carries most of a pharmaceutical company's institutional memory: documents. Whether you keep your procedures on paper in fire-proof cabinets or in a validated electronic DMS, an inspector will always, always ask for something written. That something must be correct, current, consistent, legible, retrievable, attributable, and approved—every single time.

Data integrity failures are dramatic, but document failures are embarrassingly common. One out-of-date SOP, one unsigned batch record, or one mis-matched specification can collapse months of preparation. Because documents feel familiar, we assume we have them under control—until an auditor pulls the one we forgot to update. This chapter is about shining a cold, bright light on that assumption and showing you how AI-driven review workflows can remove the blind spots that keep tripping us up.

1. Why the Document Problem Exists

1.1 Volume, Velocity, Variety

- A mid-size sterile plant typically controls 6,000–9,000 GMP-relevant documents: SOPs, WIs, forms, batch records, validation protocols, reports, specifications, labels, SDSs, job aids, training materials, change-control packages, and more.

- Every process tweak, equipment swap, or regulatory update ripples through multiple documents. A single spec change in QC can force revisions to an SOP, a batch record, and a training module—three separate owners, three separate review clocks.
- The velocity is brutal: warning-letter analyses show that sites average 35–50 document revisions per week.

1.2 Human Cognitive Limits

No matter how disciplined we are, brains fatigue. After about 25 pages of dense text or 90 minutes of intense comparison work, error rates rise exponentially. Add context switching—approving an SOP at 10:00, entering a deviation at 10:15, racing to an OOS meeting at 11:00—and blind spots multiply.

1.3 The Illusion of Second Review

We love the comforting idea that a "second pair of eyes" saves us. In practice, the second reviewer often inherits the first reviewer's cognitive framing; both miss the same subtle inconsistency. Psychologists call this "shared informational blindness." Two fatigued reviewers are not better than one well-supported reviewer.

2. How Blind Spots Cause Audit Failures

1. A batch record instructs operators to torque cap-seals to 25 ± 3 N·m. The torque wrench calibration SOP lists 25 ± 1 N·m. The mismatch is invisible until the inspector spots it and asks for your risk assessment.

2. A cleaning validation report references "SOP-HVAC-014 Rev 02," but the current SOP is at Rev 04. The report is technically invalid.
3. The water system monitoring procedure instructs weekly TOC trending, yet the electronic logbook shows a monthly review schedule. The inspector wonders which instruction operators follow.
4. Each example appears minor. Collectively, they paint a picture of a site that approves documents mechanically without truly aligning them. Inspectors translate that picture into 483 observations under "Procedures not in accordance with 21 CFR 211.22(d), 211.100(a), 211.160(a)."

3. Why Traditional Approaches Fall Short

3.1 Periodic Review Calendars

Most sites set up a three-year review cycle. Sounds reasonable until you do the math: 7,000 documents ÷ 156 weeks ≈ 45 documents per week. Teams chase dates instead of content quality. When due dates collide with inspection prep, reviewers rubber-stamp.

3.2 "Read and Understand" Training

We assign each new revision as mandatory training. Employee inboxes flood. They click through PDFs after a night shift, retaining little, silently skipping cross-references that no longer make sense.

3.3 SharePoint Searches and Excel Trackers

You can technically find any document, but you cannot see whether ten other documents cite it inconsistently. Excel can track due dates, not conceptual coherence.

3.4 Dual-Person Verification

Designating an independent second reviewer is better than nothing, yet both humans review in the same linear order and often rely on "gut feel" rather than structured comparison logic.

4. Where AI-Driven Review Genuinely Helps

Think of AI here not as a robot authoring SOPs but as a high-functioning proofreader that never sleeps, understands context, and flags mismatches across a corpus. Several capabilities make the difference:

- Natural-language similarity detection: The algorithm reads thousands of paragraphs and highlights deviations in critical statements ("25 ± 1 N·m" vs. "25 ± 3 N·m").
- Reference integrity mapping: It identifies where SOP-HVAC-014 is cited across files and alerts you if citations don't match the current rev.
- Risk-weighted review queues: Instead of a flat three-year calendar, the system scores documents by criticality and change-impact heat-maps, pushing high-risk docs to the front.
- Continuous learning from change controls: When a change control modifies a parameter, the AI automatically proposes the downstream docs that might need revision, reducing the "needle in haystack" chase.
- Semantic search: Typing "filter integrity test acceptance" retrieves not only exact keyword hits but logically related phrases ("bubble point ≤ 55 psi", "integrity pressure not to exceed 3.8 bar").

Important: these are decision-support functions. A human still decides. AI turns the flashlight onto the dark corners you forgot to examine.

5. A Practical Framework: The Five-Level Smart Review Loop

I use this loop with clients who want a regulator-credible, resource-sane path from paper chaos to AI-assisted clarity. You can adapt it to any size site.

Level 1—Capture

Digitize everything you can, but validate the scan quality. Garbage in, garbage out. For paper master batch records, a 300 dpi searchable PDF is the practical minimum.

Level 2—Contextualize

Tag each document with metadata that matters: product, process step, equipment, critical parameter, regulatory citation. Resist the urge to over-tag; five to eight tags per document is usually the sweet spot.

Level 3—Compare

Run AI similarity checks against:

- Previous revisions (to spot inadvertent wording drift)
- Sister documents (batch record vs. SOP)
- External standards (pharmacopeial monographs, CFR excerpts you legally hold copies of)

Level 4—Comment

Route flagged mismatches to SMEs. Provide them with side-by-side views and risk notes. The AI recommends but does not auto-change text.

Level 5—Close

When the SME accepts or rejects each recommendation, the decision and reasoning are logged. The loop data trains the model. Over time, false-positive rates drop, and trust rises.

6. Case Study: The Discreet Torque Mismatch

A solid-dose plant in Puerto Rico received a 483 for "Procedures not followed" because operators applied 25 ± 3 N·m torque, yet the equipment calibration spec allowed only ± 1 N·m. Management blamed the operators until they ran the corpus through a pilot AI compare engine. The mismatch traced back to an SOP rev eight months earlier that quietly broadened the tolerance to reduce cap cracks. Nobody updated the calibration spec.

Outcome after implementing the five-level loop:

- All torque-related docs re-tagged with a "Torque_Critical" label.
- Similarity scan uncovered 12 other hidden mismatches (tablet press ejector force, blister sealing temperature).
- Annual review burden dropped 37 % because only changed parameters triggered AI alerts; redundant "date-driven" reviews were waived under a risk-based rationale. The Puerto Rico site has passed two FDA inspections since without a single documentation observation.

7. Regulatory Alignment: Showing Inspectors the Logic

Inspectors do not need to love AI. They need to see that you, the human quality unit, remain in charge and are using technology to fulfill the intent of the regulations.

1. Demonstrate traceability: A simple dashboard that shows each SOP, its current rev, cross-reference count, last AI scan date, and human approval record satisfies 21 CFR 211.180(f)'s "readily available" requirement.
2. Preserve historical integrity: Never overwrite prior revs. Make the AI workspace read-only for historical documents.
3. Provide sampling evidence: When an inspector asks, "How do you ensure batch records align with current SOPs?" show a live example where the AI flagged a mismatch last month, the SME adjudicated, the document was revised, and training was reassigned.

8. Common Mistakes to Avoid

- Treating AI outputs as a rubber stamp. If you auto-accept, you re-create the blind spot—just digitized.
- Ignoring low-confidence flags. Some mismatches appear trivial, yet they teach the model context.
- Feeding the system obsolete or partial corpora. You cannot expect completeness when you give garbage.
- Running one-time "spring-clean" scans and then reverting to three-year reviews. Continuous vigilance is the point.
- Letting IT own everything. Quality must stay co-pilot; otherwise, criticality weighting drifts toward convenience, not compliance.

9. Implementation Playbook

1. Start with a "scope wedge"
   Pick one product family, one process area, or even a single

high-risk parameter class (e.g., temperatures, torques). Prove value fast.

2. Define review KPIs
   - Review cycle time (submission to approval)
   - Cross-reference mismatch count
   - Document "heat map" age (time since last AI scan)

Validate the engine

Perform a protocol similar to a macros-enabled DMS validation: IQ → OQ → PQ, with seeded mismatch challenges.

3. Train SMEs
   Run two-hour workshops on reading AI comparison reports. Teach them that "orange" means context check, not instant rewrite.
4. Present to regulators
   Include the AI review logic in site master file or quality manual addendum; keep it boring, procedural, and transparent.

10. Metrics That Matter

- First-Pass Alignment Rate (FPAR): proportion of new documents that pass AI scan without flags—measures authoring quality.
- Mismatch Aging: average calendar days a flagged mismatch sits before SME decision—signals bottlenecks.
- Cross-Reference Density: average number of links per document—higher density requires stronger AI support.
- Review Energy Saved: estimated human hours avoided per month vs. traditional word-by-word comparison. Auditors

appreciate when you reinvest saved time in floor presence and deviation investigations.

11. From "Approve and File" to "Question and Correlate"—The Mindset Shift

The real win is cultural. When reviewers expect the system to surface non-obvious inconsistencies, they become more curious thinkers. Instead of reading passively, they ask, "Why did the AI flag this?" This dialogue among people, documents, and technology breeds a healthier, blame-resistant quality culture.

12. Key Takeaways

- Document volume and human cognition limits create inevitable blind spots; audits exploit them.
- Traditional periodic reviews and dual-person verification look robust on paper but fail to detect cross-document inconsistencies.
- AI, used as a decision-support layer, excels at similarity detection, reference mapping, and risk-weighted review scheduling—areas humans handle poorly at scale.
- A Five-Level Smart Review Loop (Capture, Contextualize, Compare, Comment, Close) offers a regulator-friendly deployment roadmap.
- Implementation succeeds when quality owns the logic, SMEs adjudicate every flag, and metrics track both alignment and aging.
- The reward is not just fewer 483s; it is a workforce that thinks in correlations, not silos.

Smooth Transition to the Next Chapter

Documents are the formal memory of a pharmaceutical plant, but no matter how perfect your paperwork, real life on the shop floor will still throw surprises—equipment hiccups, environmental excursions, human lapses. When those surprises morph into deviations, CAPAs, or change controls, the stakes climb even higher. In the next chapter we will explore how AI can act as an early warning and triage ally, turning raw events into structured learning before they snowball into audit nightmares.

Chapter 10

Smart Document Review & Reducing Human Blind Spots

A Lead-In From Data Integrity

In the previous chapter we tackled raw data—chromatograms, instrument logs, electronic worksheets—and explored how AI can surface subtle integrity risks hours or days before an inspector would ever see them. If you followed the reasoning, you probably felt an immediate sense of relief: *"At least the data trail is now less scary."*

Hold that feeling.

Because the very next question inspectors ask, once the numbers look solid, is, **"Show me the document that tells operators how those numbers were generated."**

And that is where even otherwise disciplined organizations stumble. Why? Because documents are where human blind spots multiply exponentially. A single ambiguous sentence in a standard operating procedure (SOP) can invalidate the pristine data you just spent months safeguarding.

1. Why Documentation Trips Up Even the Best Teams

10.1.1 The Scale Problem

An average sterile manufacturing site maintains between 8,000 and 12,000 controlled documents—SOPs, master batch records

(MBRs), logbooks, validation protocols, risk assessments, training curricula, and so on. Even a midsize analytical lab often crosses the 3,000-document mark. The sheer number already exceeds what any one person, or even a small team, can fully comprehend in real time.

1.2 The Drift Problem

Documents live longer than most line managers. Over time they "drift" away from actual practice in small increments—an equipment upgrade here, a staffing change there—until an inspector asks a perfectly ordinary question:

"Why does this SOP still instruct operators to clean with solvent X when the line was switched to solvent Y two years ago?"

Suddenly, the site's credibility is on life support.

1.3 The Cognitive Load Problem

Every controlled document is a micro-contract with regulators. Writers must ensure the instructions are:

- Unambiguous
- Scientifically sound
- Aligned with complementary documents
- Compliant with the latest regulations, guidance, and internal policies
- Executable by the intended user group

Humans can handle three to four interacting constraints comfortably. Beyond that, error rates climb steeply—no matter how experienced the authoring or QA teams are.

1.4 The Blind Spot Nexus

Combine scale, drift, and cognitive overload, and you get a perfect incubator for blind spots: subtle gaps and inconsistencies hidden in plain sight until an outsider—often an inspector—stumbles on them.

2. Anatomy of an "Almost Perfect" SOP

Let me share an audit tale from my own files. The site in question had recently passed two client audits with praise. Their SOP for cleaning verification of a granulation suite looked flawless: slick formatting, color-coded flow diagrams, cross-references to cleaning validation reports, and traceable revision history.

On Day 2 of an EMA inspection, the assessor asked a routine question:

"How do you verify the drying oven meets the required temperature uniformity before you deem the equipment clean?"

The SOP referenced a separate protocol for temperature mapping. The assessor asked for that protocol, which in turn referenced a utility qualification report. That report cited a calibration work order from the maintenance system. When we finally traced the chain to the calibration certificate, the temperature sensors used during the original qualification had a limit of ±0.5 °C, while the SOP acceptance criterion was ±0.3 °C.

No one caught the mismatch. Not the author, not the reviewers, not even the previous auditors, because each document—looked at in isolation—was internally consistent. The mismatch only surfaced when a persistent inspector threaded the documents together.

Result: a major observation, 30-day action plan, and six months of cumulative rework. The data themselves were impeccable; the documents undermined them.

3. Traditional Document Control: Where It Helps and Where It Hinders

Document control systems—whether paper-based in lever-arch files or electronic in validated repositories—are good at:

- Version control
- Access management
- Audit trails of who approved what and when

But they struggle with:

- Semantic consistency across documents
- Detecting conflicting instructions
- Surfacing outdated references
- Highlighting ambiguous language ("as necessary," "periodically," "adequate")
- Checking underlying data assumptions (e.g., instrument capabilities vs. acceptance limits)

In other words, traditional systems manage *containers*, not *content*. They tell you the latest version exists; they do not tell you whether the words inside quietly contradict other words elsewhere.

4. Enter AI-Assisted Document Review (But Not Replacement)

4.1 The Right Kind of Intelligence

When auditors hear "AI reviewing documents," they sometimes imagine a robot rewriting procedures. That would be a regulatory nightmare. The realistic (and regulator-acceptable) approach is far narrower: AI functions as a pattern-recognition assistant that flags risk areas for human review. It is a **decision-support layer**, not an autonomous author.

4.2 Pattern Recognition Like a Seasoned Inspector

Well-trained reviewers—human reviewers—develop intuition after reading thousands of GMP documents. They spot red flags such as:

- Verb tense shifts that imply optionality
- Disappearing controls between steps
- Acceptance criteria with too many significant figures

AI can be taught to mimic that trained eye by learning from historical deviations, inspection findings, and approved document sets. It never grows tired and never loses concentration at 3 p.m. on a Friday.

4.3 Contextual Cross-Referencing

The true value appears when AI links concepts across documents. In the earlier example, an algorithm could have flagged:

"Sensor accuracy ±0.5 °C is incompatible with SOP acceptance criterion ±0.3 °C."

It surfaces a logic inconsistency, not just a spelling error.

5. Four Core Capabilities You Need

Without naming products, any AI document-review layer worth your time should provide these functions:

1. **Terminology Harmonization**
   Flag inconsistent use of critical terms (e.g., "visual inspection" vs. "macroscopic inspection").
2. **Reference Integrity Mapping**
   Trace all cross-references and confirm they point to the correct, current document version.

3. **Risk-Weighted Language Analysis**
   Identify words that add ambiguity ("routine," "as required") and rank them by risk context.
4. **Quantitative Consistency Checks**
   Compare numeric limits, units, and statistical approaches across documents to detect hidden conflicts.
5. Each capability should culminate in a **review queue** for human subject-matter experts (SMEs) to accept, reject, or further investigate the AI's findings.

6. Realistic Scenario: The Misaligned Batch Record

Let's walk through a condensed scenario to see where AI adds value without stealing human judgment.

1. A formulation scientist updates an MBR to reflect a minor change in excipient supplier.
2. The ERP system recognizes the new supplier's material specification, which has a wider moisture limit (≤5 % vs. previous ≤3 %).
3. The MBR is forwarded for QA review.
4. An AI engine performs a cross-check and discovers that the related in-process control (IPC) instruction still requires moisture testing at ≤3 %.
5. The AI flags the discrepancy and routes it to the IPC SME.
6. The SME decides the moisture limit should remain at ≤3 % because of downstream stability concerns. The correction flows back to the specification system, not the MBR.
7. Outcome: No batch initiated with conflicting limits, no deviation opened, and no audit finding. Humans made the

decision; AI ensured they saw the conflict before production began.

7. Common Mistakes to Avoid When Automating Document Review

1. **Treating AI Findings as Gospel**
   AI flags possibilities, not certainties. Blindly accepting suggestions can introduce new errors or deviate from validated state.
2. **Over-Automating Approvals**
   Auto-approving low-risk changes on the basis of AI scoring alone undermines the principle of independent QA review.
3. **Ignoring the Training Set Bias**
   If AI is trained only on legacy documents, it may reproduce outdated practices. Always include current regulatory guidance in the learning corpus.
4. **Confusing Readability with Compliance**
   Readability scores are helpful but do not guarantee scientific or regulatory soundness.
5. **Leaving SMEs Out**
   Without SME involvement, contextual nuances—such as why a limit was originally set—may be lost, leading to superficially "clean" documents that are technically wrong.

8. Building a Human + AI Review Workflow

8.1 The "Snowball" Review Cycle

Think of each new or revised document as a small snowball rolling down a hill. The longer it rolls unchallenged, the bigger—and riskier—it becomes. The workflow below prompts early friction:

- **Draft Stage** – Author runs an instantaneous AI pre-check.
- **Peer Review** – AI produces a comparison report against similar documents; peers focus on flagged deltas.
- **QA Approval** – QA sees AI's cumulative risk heat-map and focuses their energy accordingly.
- **Periodic Surveillance** – AI re-scans approved documents every night; any change in reference documents triggers alerts.

The "snowball" never grows large enough to trigger avalanches during audits.

8.2 Risk-Weighted Document Surveillance

Not all documents deserve equal monitoring. An SOP regulating aseptic interventions in Grade A areas has higher risk than a site-wide dress-code policy. Assign risk scores (high, medium, low) and let the AI tailor scan frequency:

- High Risk – Real-time surveillance
- Medium Risk – Weekly
- Low Risk – Monthly

The risk logic remains under human governance and can be updated whenever processes evolve.

9. Metrics That Actually Matter

AI vendors love exotic dashboards. Regulators do not. Focus on metrics that align with quality outcomes:

- **Discrepancies Detected Pre-Approval** – Shows proactive power
- **Time Saved in QA Review** – Indicates resource reallocation to higher-value tasks
- **Post-Implementation Deviations Linked to Document Errors** – Should trend towards zero
- **Inspector Observations Related to Documentation** – A direct measure of audit impact
- **SME Acceptance Rate of AI Recommendations** – Calibrates algorithm relevance

These metrics tell a story auditors understand: risk reduction, not gadget fascination.

10. The Mindset Shift: From Archiving to Living Documents

Historically, we wrote an SOP, filed it, and prayed no one had to pull it out before the next revision cycle. AI-supported review flips that paradigm. Documents become **living risk artefacts**—monitored, interrogated, and improved continually. That mindset requires cultural change:

- Authors must accept continuous feedback loops.
- QA becomes a risk curator, not merely a gatekeeper.
- SMEs evolve from one-time reviewers to lifecycle owners.

When inspectors see evidence of active surveillance—monthly risk reports, logged resolutions, trend analyses—they perceive a mature quality culture. Observations drop, sometimes to zero, not because defects vanish but because **they are captured upstream**.

11. Key Takeaways

1. Documentation blind spots are the silent killers of otherwise compliant operations.
2. Traditional document control secures versions but leaves content conflicts undetected.
3. AI excels at pattern recognition and cross-referencing yet must remain a decision-support layer.
4. Build workflows where AI flags, humans decide, and QA validates the risk assessment.
5. Measure success by reduced discrepancies, not by how many pages the algorithm scans.
6. A living-document mindset signals maturity to regulators and protects both company and careers.
7. A Bridge to the Next Chapter

We have dealt with proactive surveillance of the words that guide our processes. But what happens when, despite our best preventive measures, reality diverges from the documented path? Deviations, CAPAs, and change controls become the next frontline. In the following chapter we will explore how AI can keep those essential quality systems from spiraling into chaos—and how it can do so without ever writing a single deviation on your behalf.

Chapter 11

How Careers Get Damaged During Audits

A Quiet Corridor After the Audit—And the Whisper You Never Forget

The inspection team has just left the conference room. The site head thanks everyone for "pulling together." People disperse. You step into the corridor to catch your breath—and overhear two inspectors talking in lowered voices.

"Good scientist. Shame about the documentation."

They are talking about you.

I have been in that corridor myself, and I can tell you that a single comment—spoken after the binders, power-points, and closing meetings—can echo through an entire career. The corrective and preventive actions will be documented, the deviation will get its CAPA plan, but your name, fairly or unfairly, is now associated with a finding.

This chapter is about that unseen cost: how inspections damage individual careers—sometimes permanently—even when companies recover. We will examine the mechanisms that lead from a citation on paper to a setback in someone's professional life, and then look at how AI-assisted practices can create a personal safety net without falling into techno-utopian promises.

1. Why Audit Findings Become Personal Even When They Sound Procedural

1.1 The Human Face Behind Every SOP

Regulators do not intend to single out individuals; nevertheless, every observation has an origin. When a laboratory chromatography file is missing an audit trail entry, inspectors ask, "Who performed the injection?" That name becomes part of the narrative even if it never appears in the form 483. Over time, organizations informally attach reputational labels:

- "Reliable analyst"
- "Documentation risk"
- "Good under pressure but lacks detail"

Those labels influence promotions, project assignments, and leadership opportunities far more than people admit in official performance reviews.

1.2 The Shadow CV

Because the pharmaceutical industry is heavily networked, word travels across sites and companies. I call it the "shadow CV." It contains all the unwritten notes your formal résumé never shows: how you handled that unplanned deviation at 2 a.m., whether you argued with the inspector, whether your batch record backlog ballooned. Recruiters and hiring managers, who themselves survived audits, tune into this informal frequency.

1.3 Regulatory Memory Is Long

One might think that after a successful re-inspection the past evaporates. It does not. When inspectors return, they often begin with the last inspection's close-out letter. If your name was attached to an issue then, you may have to answer for it again. Careers erode not by a single blow but by repeated small abrasions of credibility.

2. Mechanisms of Career Damage During and After Audits

Let's get precise about how personal risk materializes. I've tracked five repeatable pathways.

2.1 The "Signature on Everything" Trap

Well-meaning managers ask high performers to sign multiple forms to "get things moving." Eventually an inspector notices identical handwriting across unrelated operations. Their inference: possible rubber-stamping. Even if each record is valid, the individual is now viewed as reckless with data integrity.

2.2 The Email Archaeology Effect

During audits, inspectors request contemporaneous evidence. Quality teams scramble through email threads to locate approvals or clarifications. Casual wording—"we'll clean it up later" or "just override the alarm"—can be interpreted as intent. Once projected on the inspection room screen, that email becomes indelible. The sender's professional judgment is publicly questioned.

2.3 The Escalation Bypass

Consider a production supervisor who reroutes a deviation directly to operations management, bypassing QA to "save time." If uncovered, the event is treated as a governance gap. The individual's decision-making is cast as non-compliant, affecting future leadership roles.

2.4 The Over-Commit Syndrome

In closing meetings, some technical leads promise corrective actions faster than physically possible. Weeks later, corporate quality struggles to deliver. The discrepancy is reported back to regulators, and the original promiser is tagged as unreliable.

2.5 The Silence Misinterpretation

Not speaking up can be as harmful as speaking incorrectly. Analysts who know the root cause of an excursion but stay silent in front of auditors—perhaps awaiting managerial clearance—appear evasive. Inspectors record "lack of adequate knowledge or training," which reflects directly on competence.

3. Why Traditional Audit-Preparation Approaches Fail to Protect Individuals

Organizations pour effort into readiness checklists, mock audits, and documentation blitzes. Yet individuals still absorb collateral damage. Where is the disconnect?

3.1 Checklists Are Site-Level, Risk Is Person-Level

Corporate readiness focuses on systems: validation status, SOP revisions, training matrices. Personal vulnerabilities—like a lone scientist carrying too many batch reviews—hide beneath aggregated KPIs.

3.2 Fire-Drill Culture Overlooks Routine Behavior

In the final 30 days before an announced inspection, behaviors sharpen: every date, every initial is double-checked. But inspectors look for habits, not sprints. They sample records from six months ago—exactly when the everyday shortcuts happened.

3.3 Coaching, Not Training, Is Missing

Employees attend GMP refreshers but rarely receive coaching on how to communicate with inspectors, how to pace answers, how to handle uncertain data. The moment pressure mounts, they revert to defensive postures, which inspectors read as concealment.

3.4 Data Overload Conceals Accountability

Manual recordkeeping generates mountains of data, and senior staff cannot reasonably review everything. Fault lines appear under the weight of paperwork. When an error surfaces, fingers point at whoever last touched the document—even if systemic workload was the true root cause.

4. Where AI and Intelligent Automation Provide Personal Career Protection

Before diving in, recall our book's stance: AI is a decision-support and risk-visibility layer, not a replacement for human judgment. With that boundary, let's see how properly scoped automation buffers individuals from the five damage pathways identified earlier.

4.1 Digital Lineage Clarifies Genuine Responsibility

Modern systems can automatically capture who created, modified, reviewed, and approved each data element, down to time-stamped keystrokes. This immutable lineage does two things:

- Shields conscientious employees from blanket blame by showing exact involvement
- Surfaces role overload (e.g., one user approving five steps in a row) so managers can redistribute tasks before audit day

By making accountability transparent, AI prevents the "signature on everything" trap from forming in the first place.

4.2 Context-Aware Communication Review

Natural-language processing, when embedded in corporate email or messaging archives, can flag phrases that historically correlate with compliance risks ("clean it up later," "just back-date"). Early alerts allow senders to clarify or correct wording immediately rather than months later in an inspection room. Importantly, such systems operate internally; nothing is transmitted externally. You remain in control of your narrative.

4.3 Escalation Guardrails

Workflow engines augmented with decision rules prevent deviations from skipping mandatory QA steps. If someone attempts to bypass, the system blocks submission and automatically documents the attempt. Instead of punishing after the fact, the platform guides correct behavior upfront, preserving both compliance and individual reputation.

4.4 Promise Realism Analytics

When drafting CAPA timelines, AI can evaluate historical performance data—average equipment downtime, validation lead times, supplier responsiveness—and suggest realistic completion dates. Over-committing becomes less likely because the system provides evidence-based projections in real time.

4.5 Adaptive Coaching Interfaces

Conversational AI modules can simulate inspector questioning, tailoring scenarios to a user's role and recent data. Unlike generic mock audits, these simulations pull actual SOP changes and deviation logs to create realistic drills. Employees practice answering tough questions, receive feedback on clarity and completeness, and enter real inspections with muscle memory rather than stage fright.

5. Common Missteps When Implementing AI for Individual Protection

Introducing technology is itself fraught with risks. Here are pitfalls I've witnessed firsthand:

- Treating AI alerts as disciplinary triggers instead of coaching opportunities. The moment people feel surveilled rather than supported, they game the system or disengage, nullifying its protective value.

- Ignoring algorithmic bias. If models flag certain communication styles more often (e.g., non-native English phrasing), you can inadvertently stigmatize specific groups. Always validate alert thresholds across demographics.
- Over-automating sign-offs. Some companies configure systems to auto-approve low-risk steps, thinking it frees experts for critical tasks. In practice, it creates opaque decision paths inspectors cannot trace, undermining individual as well as organizational credibility.
- Leaving out context in audit trails. Raw keystrokes without human-readable rationales confuse inspectors and users alike. Always pair automated lineage with plain-language descriptions.

6. A Practical Framework: The Personal Risk Heat-Map

Below is a step-by-step process I coach professionals to adopt. It translates systemic audit-readiness into personal career insurance.

Step 1 – Inventory Your Audit-Touch Points
List every record, form, or data entry where your name appears as creator, reviewer, or approver. Include digital and paper systems.

Step 2 – Classify Each Touch Point by Failure Visibility
Ask: "If this item were out of spec, how quickly would an inspector find it?" Routine batch records are high-visibility; internal meeting notes are lower.

Step 3 – Overlay Automation Coverage
Mark which items already have AI-enabled safeguards (lineage,

anomaly detection, workflow guardrails) and which rely solely on manual diligence.

Step 4 – Assign Personal Risk Scores
Combine visibility and automation coverage into a 1-to-5 scale. High visibility + low automation = score 5 (red zone).

Step 5 – Prioritize Self-Checks
Schedule brief, recurring reviews of red-zone items. Use system-generated dashboards where possible; where not, do structured spot-checks.

Step 6 – Document Preventive Actions
For each high-risk area, write a two-sentence "what I do to stay clean" note. Store it in a personal log. If ever questioned, you can demonstrate foresight.

Step 7 – Update Quarterly
Audits can be announced or surprise. Quarterly updates keep the map current but avoid administrative overload.

7. A True Story—Names Changed, Lessons Preserved

Marianne was a senior validation engineer at a European sterile-fill facility. During an unannounced inspection, regulators discovered temperature mapping raw data missing for a critical warehouse. The site produced a validation summary report, signed by Marianne, stating that "all sensors recorded within limits."

The inspector's forensics team recovered partial sensor logs showing a 10-hour excursion. Marianne argued she never saw those raw files; she had relied on an emailed spreadsheet from a junior colleague. The observation escalated into a major finding.

Here is how AI could have altered the outcome:

- Raw Data Ingest: An automated pipeline would have linked raw sensor output directly to the validation report, making it impossible to sign off without seeing complete data.
- Anomaly Alert: A simple out-of-range flag could have triggered before report compilation.
- Responsibility Matrix: The system would show that Marianne received incomplete data, shifting accountability to the data preparer, not the approver.

Instead, her credibility suffered; she was reassigned to a non-critical role for 18 months. The company fixed the system, but Marianne bore the personal cost.

8. Mindset Shift: From Defensive Posture to Proactive Transparency

Inspectors do not aim to ruin careers; they aim to protect patients. The best defense is to become a living example of the quality culture you talk about in SOPs. AI tools help, but the mindset must precede the tooling.

- Own your data trail. Before signing, ask yourself, "If someone questions this in two years, can I explain every value?" If not, pause.
- Embrace alerts as allies, not annoyances. A late-night system ping may save you from a public explanation later.
- Seek visibility, not shelter. Volunteer for dashboards that show your metrics; transparency is a career asset during audits.

9. Key Takeaways

1. Audit findings invariably attach to people, not just processes. The informal "shadow CV" influences careers across companies.
2. Traditional readiness efforts focus on systems, leaving personal vulnerabilities unaddressed.
3. AI can protect individuals by recording transparent lineage, coaching communication, enforcing workflow guardrails, and providing data-driven realistic commitments.
4. Misuse of AI—surveillance, bias, over-automation—can create new risks. Design with coaching, fairness, and traceability in mind.
5. A Personal Risk Heat-Map gives every professional a structured way to monitor and reduce their audit-related career exposure.

10. Looking Ahead—From Personal Survival to Collective Resilience

In the next chapter, we will flip the perspective: instead of shielding individual careers, how do we deploy AI as a personal safety net that uplifts everyone without diminishing accountability? We will explore how to align personal and organizational incentives so that "audit survival" evolves into "audit excellence," making each inspection less about defense and more about demonstrating the robustness of our shared systems.

Chapter 12

AI for Deviations, CAPAs & Change Controls

The Quiet Pivot From Static Documents to Living Quality Events

In the previous chapter we walked through how AI can surface discrepancies that hide in plain sight inside controlled documents. Documents, however, only tell half of the story. The other half is written every day in deviation reports, CAPA files, and change-control records—the living, breathing evidence of how your organisation actually responds when things go off-script.

Auditors love this evidence because it strips away theatre. A batch record can look flawless, but if the same filling line shows a string of recurring deviations, or if CAPAs close suspiciously fast with no follow-up effectiveness checks, the inspector will politely nod at your SOP binder and then focus on those event files. Time and again I see well-intentioned teams stumble here. Not because they are careless or untrained, but because deviation and change data grows faster than they can read, classify, trend, and act.

That's where AI, used correctly, can transform audit risk from a reactive scramble to a managed signal. In this chapter, we will unpack exactly how.

1. Why Deviations, CAPAs, and Change Controls Are Audit Landmines

Deviations, CAPAs, and change controls (I will simply call them "quality events" for brevity) share three characteristics that make them irresistible—sometimes fatal—fishing ponds for auditors:

1. They represent unscripted reality.
2. They cut across silos (manufacturing, QC, engineering, IT, validation, supply chain).
3. They multiply rapidly; each event spawns more data than most teams can retire gracefully.
4. Let's look at each in turn.

1.1 Unscripted Reality

A deviation cannot be pre-rehearsed. The language is raw, the root causes often messy, and the closure justification either sincere or suspiciously polished. Auditors know this, which is why they open the deviation log first. If the narrative feels sanitised, their suspicion meter jumps.

1.2 Cross-Functional Complexity

A single OOS result might trigger an investigation, a production hold, a qualification re-run, supplier queries, a software patch, and multiple CAPAs. Every handoff introduces interpretation gaps and data integrity risks. Even in mature sites, the paper or PDF trail can resemble a detective board connected by red strings rather than a coherent story.

1.3 Exponential Growth

A 200-person facility can easily generate 1,000 deviations and 400 change controls a year, each with several attachments, approvals, and deadlines. Multiply that by global sites and you enter the territory where tribal memory fails, spreadsheets break, and management dashboards lag weeks behind reality.

2. How the Problem Blossoms Into Audit Findings

Auditors rarely cite "too many deviations" as a violation. Instead they conclude:

- Root-cause analysis is superficial.
- Repeat deviations show the CAPA system is ineffective.
- Change-control risk assessments are inconsistent.
- Data integrity lapses (back-dated entries, missing signatures) demonstrate a broken quality culture.

The visible symptom—late closures, missing effectiveness checks, stale change controls—traces back to one systemic weakness: humans are relying on manual reading, sorting, and trending of unstructured text. By the time someone notices a pattern, the inspector is already on site.

A favourite 483 phrase—"failure to identify adverse trends in a timely manner"—is essentially a polite way of saying, "You had the data, but nobody was looking at it in time."

3. Traditional Approaches and Their Shortfalls

Over the past two decades, companies have tried four main tactics to tame quality-event chaos:

1. Bigger teams: Hire more QA reviewers.
2. Periodic trending: Export data to Excel each quarter for KPI slides.
3. Workflow software: Deploy an electronic QMS to enforce fields and signatures.

4. Lean/Six Sigma projects: Map the process, remove waste, standardise templates.
5. Each tactic helps, but none addresses the cognitive bottleneck—the human effort to read every narrative, detect subtle connections, and judge risk objectively. Let's dissect why.

3.1 Bigger Teams, Smaller Insight

A review queue can definitely be emptied by adding staff. But if complexity grows faster than headcount, reviewers skim. Skimming invites confirmation bias ("I think I've seen this before, so closure looks OK"), and the real signal hides under volume.

3.2 Periodic Trending = Retrospective Shock

Quarterly dashboards are historical documents that show what you no longer can fix. By the time the CAPA trend line spikes, the initial deviation root causes have aged and institutional memory is hazy.

3.3 Workflow Software: Compliance Hygiene, Not Intelligence

Most eQMS platforms enforce completion of required steps; they do not infer whether the steps are meaningful. The system may demand five Why's, but it cannot judge if the fifth Why is a genuine system cause or a politely phrased shrug.

3.4 Lean Projects Fade When Champions Move On

I've led enough Kaizen events to value their power, yet the sustainability problem remains: once the black belts rotate, the meticulously colour-coded war room charts simmer quietly in storage.

In summary, classic solutions attack the pipeline, not the cognition. AI offers a lever precisely on that cognition gap—but only if implemented with humility.

4. Where AI Genuinely Adds Value

Let's ground the promise. AI cannot write your CAPAs for you, nor should it approve change controls. It can, however, surface patterns, suggest priorities, and project risk in ways exponentially faster than human scanning. Done well, it becomes a decision-support co-pilot that releases human experts to perform the nuanced judgment regulators expect.

Below are seven high-impact areas you can explore without falling into hype.

4.1 Real-Time Deviation Triage

Natural Language Processing (NLP) models can read deviation narration and classify the event into risk brackets within seconds. Think of it as an early-warning radar. The QA reviewer still reads the file, but now starts with a risk prediction instead of a blank page. Statistical back-testing shows triage accuracy often beats inexperienced reviewers and matches senior QA staff consistency.

Key Benefits

- High-risk events jump to the front of the queue.
- Recurring problem statements are flagged automatically ("particle observed" appears 12 times this month).
- Low-risk, well-documented events can flow faster, reducing backlog.

4.2 Suggested Root-Cause Paths

Pattern-matching algorithms can highlight plausible root-cause candidates based on similar historical events. For example, if previous deviations citing "intermittent pressure drop" were traced to diaphragm valve wear, the system nudges the investigator to inspect that angle early. It does not replace the 5-Why session; it shortens the search.

4.3 CAPA Effectiveness Forecasting

Machine-learning models trained on past CAPAs can estimate the probability that a proposed action plan will prevent recurrence within a set horizon. Factors include action type, implementation time, and whether training alone historically sufficed. This turns the "We'll see in six months" gamble into a quantified risk discussion at closure meetings.

4.4 Duplicate CAPA Detection

Large firms accidently open multiple CAPAs for the same systemic cause. Text-similarity analysis alerts teams when new CAPAs overlap with existing ones, reducing redundancy and auditor irritation at seeing three open plans for an identical HVAC issue.

4.5 Change-Control Impact Assessment

AI can map proposed changes against past deviations, batch yields, and maintenance logs to forecast potential ripple effects. Imagine a pop-up that says, "This minor process change has historically correlated with a 40 % spike in sterility-test failures if not accompanied by retraining." Decision makers gain foresight instead of hindsight.

4.6 Backlog Risk Heat-Mapping

Visual AI dashboards turn thousands of open actions into a heat map ranked by overdue status, risk category, and patient impact. Leadership can allocate resources surgically rather than chasing whatever the weekly meeting highlights.

4.7 Continuous Learning Feedback Loops

Because AI models improve with data, each closed deviation or CAPA updates the system's understanding of failure modes. Over time the algorithm becomes a living knowledge base far richer than tribal memory, yet always ready for a human challenge.

5. A Case Study—From Firefighting to Forecasting

Walk with me into a sterile injectables plant I assisted last year. The site had an electronic QMS but faced a 120-day deviation closure backlog and three repeat deviations highlighted across two inspections. Management asked for "some AI thing" to fix it, and I gave my usual disclaimer: AI is headlights, not brakes. They agreed.

5.1 Baseline Pain

- 1,870 open deviations, 27 % overdue.
- Average closure time: 94 days (SOP target 30).
- 18 repeat deviations in last FDA audit.
- CAPA approval board drowning in 150 ageing action plans.

5.2 Intervention Steps

1. Data Curation: We extracted five years of deviation narratives, linked them to CAPA actions and closure outcomes, scrubbed personal identifiers, and tagged final root-cause categories.
2. Model Training: A supervised NLP model learned to classify deviation risk on a three-level scale (critical, major, minor).
3. Pilot Deployment: For six weeks, reviewers received the AI risk score along with a list of similar past deviations and their successful CAPAs.
4. Human Override Mechanism: Reviewers could accept or reject the AI suggestion, and the choice fed back into model refinement.
5. Dashboarding: A live funnel displayed how many days each deviation waited before first human touch, broken down by risk tier.

5.3 Results After 4 Months

- Average first-touch time dropped from nine days to under 24 hours.
- Critical-risk deviation backlog cleared; only minor events remained overdue.
- Repeat deviations fell by 56 %.
- CAPA board meetings focused on five high-impact actions instead of 30 agenda items.

5.4 Inspector Feedback

During the subsequent EMA inspection, the lead GMP inspector commented, "Your deviation triage has matured—issues appear prioritised and recurring themes well addressed." No observation was issued in this area.

Remember: no code was written by QA; IT hosted the model, QA fed the data, and humans kept authority on every decision.

6. Common Missteps to Avoid

AI projects in quality event management often stumble for predictable reasons. Forewarned is forearmed.

1. Dirty Data In, Faster Confusion Out
   If narratives are copied-and-pasted boilerplate, the model learns nothing. Enforce unique, specific deviation entries.
2. "AI Wrote My CAPA" Syndrome
   Tempting as it is, regulators still want human reasoning. Use AI to recommend, not author, root-cause statements.
3. Black-Box Phobia
   If QA cannot explain, at a high level, why the model ranked a

deviation "critical," auditors will doubt its credibility. Model interpretability tools are a must.

4. Over-Automation
   Routing every low-risk deviation to auto-closure is alluring but dangerous. Spot-check a statistically valid sample—or risk Missing Something Big.
5. Starving the Model
   Quality events are often shielded by confidentiality. Without enough historical examples, predictions will be noisy. Start small, expand gradually.
6. Ignoring Change-Management Impact
   Introducing AI alters job descriptions. Involve reviewers early to prevent quiet resistance that sabotages adoption.

7. A Practical Framework—The R.A.I.S.E. Model

Drawing on projects across four continents, I distilled a five-step implementation approach whose acronym reflects the goal: to RAISE the maturity of your deviation and CAPA process.

1. Record with Precision
   - Insist on clear, structured deviation narratives.
   - Discourage "copy-paste" from earlier templates.
2. Assess Using Hybrid Intelligence
   - Let AI score risk and surface similar events.
   - Require human reviewers to confirm or revise.
3. Integrate Across Systems
   - Connect deviation data with maintenance logs, LIMS, batch records.
   - The more context, the smarter the suggestion engine.

4. Supervise the Algorithm
   - Monitor false positives/negatives monthly.
   - Retrain models when process changes significantly alter data patterns.
5. Evolve the Culture
   - Share success stories and lessons widely.
   - Embed AI literacy in QA onboarding, demystifying the black box.
6. Follow these steps cyclically, not linearly. Every iteration should compress review times while improving insight depth.

8. Ethical and Regulatory Guardrails

AI applied to quality events touches patient safety and data integrity—the heart of GMP. Regulators are clear: delegation of critical thinking to unvalidated black boxes is unacceptable.

Keep these guardrails in mind:

- Validation
  Treat the AI model as a category of software requiring documented requirements, risk assessment, and ongoing verification. You needn't freeze the model as a static entity, but you must document how it learns and how you know learning is beneficial.
- Data Privacy
  De-identify personal names in deviation narratives before feeding them to training sets. This is not just GDPR courtesy; it prevents bias ("John is always at fault").
- Explainability
  Provide inspectors with a plain-language explanation of

model factors—e.g., "High frequency of 'sterility failure' plus short interval between events equals elevated risk score."

- Human Oversight
  A clear SOP must state that AI recommendations are advisory. Final disposition remains a human prerogative, documented and auditable.
- Continuous Monitoring
  Build KPI triggers to detect model drift. If the proportion of critical events drops suspiciously overnight, pause auto-routing and investigate.

9. Transitioning to the Next Frontier

We have travelled from firefighting deviations to forecasting them. Yet technology alone does not make an organisation audit-proof. It needs people who understand how to interrogate AI insights and leaders who cultivate psychological safety for raising concerns.

In the next chapter we will focus squarely on humans—how careers get damaged during audits and how, if you weave AI responsibly into your personal workflow, it can become a safety net rather than a threat. The mechanics we discussed here set the technical foundation; the upcoming chapter takes us into the human dimension where audit survival ultimately succeeds or fails.

Key Takeaways

- Quality events reveal the unfiltered truth of GMP performance; auditors scrutinise them intensely.
- Manual review processes buckle under the volume and complexity of deviations, CAPAs, and change controls.
- AI can triage risk, suggest root-cause paths, forecast CAPA effectiveness, and map change-control impact—always as decision support, never as autonomous authority.
- Success depends on clean data, explainability, vigilant human oversight, and cultural adoption, not on flashy algorithms.
- The R.A.I.S.E. framework—Record, Assess, Integrate, Supervise, Evolve—offers a pragmatic roadmap to embed AI into your quality-event process while satisfying regulatory expectations.

Chapter 13

Making AI Regulator-Friendly

A Quick Look Back—and a Hard Look Forward

In the previous chapter we talked about AI as your personal safety net, the invisible colleague who spots the things you missed at 2 a.m. and politely whispers, "Check this before the inspector sees it." That individual focus was deliberate: careers are made—or broken—one decision at a time.

Now we zoom out from the individual to the organization. It's one thing to run a smart algorithm on your laptop and get a useful signal; it's a very different thing to run that same algorithm under the fluorescent lights of an inspection room while three regulators flip through your deviation log.

The question this chapter answers is blunt:

"How do I make sure the AI that helps me **also** helps me survive the inspection?"

The short answer is: make AI regulator-friendly.

The long answer follows.

1. Why "Regulator-Friendly" Even Matters

I've sat on both sides of the table: once as the plant QA head struggling to explain a new automated analytics platform, and later as the consultant hired to clean up the 483 that platform helped create. The root cause in both cases was the same:

1. We treated AI as a technology project, not a compliance system.
2. We assumed regulators would see the obvious benefits.
3. We documented "enough"—but in ways that made sense only to us.
4. Regulator-friendly AI is not softer, smaller, or slower AI. It's AI wrapped in a compliance shell the inspector can pierce, examine, and accept. Anything less becomes a black box—and black boxes spark 483s faster than data-integrity macros ever did.

2. How "Unfriendly" AI Triggers Audit Failures

Inspectors are not out to ban innovation, but they are professionally trained to assume the worst until proven otherwise. When they face an AI system, three red flags pop up immediately.

1. **Opaque Logic**
   If the output changes from batch to batch and no one can trace the logic path, they see an uncontrolled process.
2. **Validation Gaps**
   Traditional validation scripts expect deterministic outputs. AI rarely obliges, producing probabilities instead of binary pass/fail. The mismatch looks like inadequate validation.
3. **Lifecycle Blind Spots**
   AI improves with data drifts and model retraining—exactly the sort of changes regulators expect you to document and control. If you can't articulate that lifecycle in simple, static terms, trust evaporates.

4. Put simply, an AI-centered failure is rarely about malicious intent. It's about unmanaged uncertainty. And audits punish uncertainty.

3. Why Traditional Approaches Fall Short

You cannot staple a standard IQ/OQ/PQ protocol onto a continuously learning system and expect compliance blessings. I've watched teams try. The results fall into two patterns:

- **Over-Documentation Paralysis**
  They write 800-page validation reports no one reads. The inspection ends with a polite 483 note: "Documentation fails to demonstrate evidence of control."
- **Minimalist Wishful Thinking**
  They assume "industry standard" tools need no validation. The inspector reads one vendor brochure, raises an eyebrow, and writes, "Lack of software validation per 21 CFR Part 11."

What's missing in both approaches is alignment: the validation logic must mirror regulators' mental model of risk, not the vendor's slide deck or the data scientist's Jupyter notebook.

4. Where AI Actually Helps the Regulator—If You Let It

Paradoxically, AI can make an inspector's life easier. Done right, it offers:

- Faster traceability between raw data, decisions, and actions.
- Statistically sound detection of data or process drift.
- Clear, time-stamped, tamper-evident logs that prove you saw issues before they became 483s.

Those strengths, however, surface only when the system is designed with audit questions in mind.

5. The Six Principles of Regulator-Friendly AI

Below is the framework I teach clients when they want AI without anxiety. Use it as a checklist, a design compass, and a conversation starter with your cross-functional teams.

1. Explainability Over Mystery

If you understand it only because the vendor demo looked cool, you don't understand it.

- Demand plain-language model summaries.
- Maintain "why-files" that map inputs → intermediate logic → outputs.
- Provide line-of-sight from each AI alert to a tangible GMP requirement.

2. Risk-Based Validation, Not Blanket Validation

Validation doesn't die in the AI age; it evolves.

- Define the model's "intended use" as precisely as you would a balance or an incubator.
- Validate the data pipeline (ingestion, preprocessing) separately from the algorithm.
- Use statistical confidence intervals as acceptance criteria instead of binary pass/fail thresholds when appropriate.

3. Controlled Learning and Change Management

An algorithm that updates weekly is a new system every week—unless you manage that learning.

- Version-lock training data sets and retain them for the product lifecycle.
- Treat retraining events as controlled changes, with documented rationale, risk assessment, and approval.
- Maintain a rollback plan as you would for any critical infrastructure.

4. Data Governance as a First-Class Citizen

AI quality = data quality × governance maturity.

- Classify data sources by GxP criticality (e.g., critical manufacturing vs. auxiliary environmental feeds).
- Enforce audit trails on data preprocessing steps—no invisible hands cleaning data.
- Periodically reconcile model inputs with their original physical or electronic sources.

5. Human-In-the-Loop Decision Rights

Regulators expect accountable humans, not algorithms, to own final decisions.

- Configure AI to recommend, not decide.
- Capture evidence that qualified personnel reviewed, accepted, or overruled each key recommendation.
- Train reviewers to spot algorithmic bias, over-fitting, and false positives—basic statistical hygiene is now a GMP skill.

6. Ethical Alignment and Bias Monitoring

What you might consider a "performance boost" can look like data tampering in hindsight.

- Validate that the model's feature selection doesn't leak sensitive or irrelevant attributes.

- Run periodic bias audits: does the algorithm unwittingly downgrade batches produced on night shifts?
- Document remediations just as you would for any out-of-specification result.

These six principles combine into one overarching mandate: Make every machine-generated insight traceable, testable, and reversible by human experts.

6. A Day in the Life—A Practical Walk-Through

Let me offer a composite story, stitched from three plants I've worked with. Names and details are altered, obviously, but the flow is authentic.

13.7.1. Morning Meeting: The Model Flag

At 9:05 a.m., the deviation dashboard flashes amber for Batch JQ-211. The AI notes a subtle correlation between a pH drift in the second fermenter and a recently calibrated probe. No spec breach occurred, but historical data suggests a 32 % likelihood of microbial deviation downstream.

The production supervisor, Maria, clicks the alert. She sees:

- Model version: v3.6.2 (validated Sept 1)
- Training data set: 167 historical fermentation runs (source locked)
- Confidence interval: 95 %

She acknowledges the alert, triggers a "review required" task, and calls QA.

Mid-Day Review: The Human Lens

QA lead Ahmed reviews the raw fermenter data, cross-references calibration logs, and decides the risk classification is "minor but credible." He documents that assessment and instructs Operations to increase sampling frequency.

Afternoon Huddle: The Regulator's Imaginary Chair

Ahmed also generates the "why-file" summary. It shows:

- Input variables considered (dissolved oxygen, pH, stirrer speed, probe history)
- Weighted contributions (pH drift 62 %, probe drift 21 %, minor variables 17 %)
- Historic comparator batches

He stores the summary under /QMS/AI/Batch-Alerts/2025/Q1.

If an inspector walked in tomorrow, Ahmed could click three links and answer: What alerted, why, who reviewed it, and what you did about it. That, in a nutshell, is regulator-friendly AI.

7. Common Mistakes to Avoid

Even mature organizations stumble over remarkably similar obstacles. If you can dodge these, you're already ahead.

1. **Outsourcing Responsibility**
   "The vendor will validate." No. The vendor validates software performance; you validate *use*.
2. **Infinite Pilot Mode**
   Running AI in "pilot" for 18 months to dodge validation only signals you can't control your tech.
3. **One-Shot Validation**
   Validating at go-live and never revisiting. Regulators know models drift; pretending otherwise invites citations.
4. **Confusing Cybersecurity with Data Integrity**
   An encrypted model is not automatically compliant. Integrity

is about accurate, complete, and retrievable data, not merely protected data.

5. **Lack of Cross-Functional Governance**
   Leaving AI governance to IT or Data Science alone ignores the QA and RA perspectives. A triad approach—IT, Data Science, QA—is mandatory.

8. The AI–GxP Alignment Canvas

When time is tight, I use a one-page visual I call the AI–GxP Alignment Canvas. It forces teams to think holistically and keeps projects honest.

- **Intended Use** – Single sentence describing the decision or insight produced.
- **Regulatory Touchpoints** – List of CFR, EMA, ICH clauses implicated.
- **Data Lineage** – Source → Transformation → Storage → Model Input.
- **Validation Strategy** – Performance metrics, acceptance criteria, worst-case scenarios.
- **Change Control Hooks** – Triggers that require retraining or revalidation.
- **Human Oversight Nodes** – Who reviews which outputs, how often, with what documented outcomes.
- **Retrospective Metrics** – How will you judge the model in production (e.g., false-positive rate < 5 %).

Filling this canvas forces early identification of blind spots that otherwise surface as audit-day panic.

A Note on Global Regulatory Nuances

USFDA focuses heavily on data integrity and decision traceability. EMA echoes those concerns but tends to ask more about lifecycle management. MHRA, fresh off multiple data-integrity scandals, digs into raw data storage and retrievability. Designing for the strictest common denominator usually covers everyone—but keep your Quality Intelligence function active, monitoring new guidance. AI is moving; regulators are jogging to keep up.

9. Building Trust—One Dialogue at a Time

Don't wait until a pre-approval inspection to reveal your shiny algorithm. Proactively engage regulators:

- Include AI elements in annual product reviews.
- When filing a variation or a PAS, add a summary of AI-assisted controls.
- Invite inspectors (virtually, if needed) to walkthroughs of your monitoring dashboards.

Early transparency decreases the aura of mystery. And regulators remember.

10. Mindset Shift: From Proof to Story

Traditional validation is proof: "We did X, it works, here's evidence." AI validation is also story: "Here's why we built it, how it learns, and when it might fail."

You're narrating a journey from raw data to safeguarded patient, with checkpoints regulators can audit. If you master that story, the proof writes itself.

11. Key Takeaways

- Regulator-friendly AI is designed around audit questions, not vendor capabilities.
- Opaque logic, validation gaps, and unmanaged model changes are the top red flags.
- Apply six principles—Explainability, Risk-Based Validation, Controlled Learning, Data Governance, Human-in-the-Loop, Ethical Alignment—to tame those flags.
- Use practical tools like the AI–GxP Alignment Canvas to align cross-functional teams early.
- Engage regulators proactively; transparency is the antidote to black-box fear.

Seamless Transition to the Next Chapter

You now have the blueprint for AI systems auditors won't fear. But blueprints mean little if the people using the tools still think in paper-based terms. In the next chapter we'll tackle that head-on—training people to think, not just click. Because ultimately, regulator-friendly AI is useless without regulator-ready humans.

Chapter 14

Training People to Think, Not Just Click

A Quick Look Back—From Regulator-Friendly Technology to Regulator-Ready People

In the last chapter we dismantled the belief that "regulator-friendly" simply means buying audit-safe software. We saw how inspectors interrogate the intent, configuration, and governance behind every algorithm you deploy. If Part 5 were a building, Chapter 13 installed the walls; Chapter 14 now installs the wiring—the human capability that brings those walls to life.

An organization can own the most defensible AI platform in the industry and still fail spectacularly if the people who feed, interpret, and act on that platform remain stuck in checkbox compliance. Inspectors are not impressed by dashboards alone; they probe the human decisions behind them. That is why the true competitive advantage is not technical firepower but cognitive firepower—people trained to think, not just click.

1. Why "Click Training" Became the Default

Pharma's training paradigm drifted toward click-through modules for three interrelated reasons:

1. **Regulatory recordability** – Learning Management Systems (LMS) produce date-stamped proof that "training occurred."

Those PDFs satisfy procedural requirements, so companies equated logs with learning.

2. **Operational urgency** – Manufacturing schedules rarely allow deep classroom time. Slide decks followed by online quizzes seem faster.
3. **Technology optimism** – Once MES, LIMS, or QMS went digital, management assumed that system prompts would guide correct behavior, reducing the need for conceptual understanding.
4. The convenient by-product is large volumes of training records—exactly the evidence auditors request. Unfortunately, inspectors quickly spot when competence was never built beneath those signatures.

2. Consequences in the Audit Room

Think back to any tense close-out meeting you have attended. How often did the conversation deteriorate like this?

Inspector: *"Show me how the analyst knew which calibration curve to accept."*
Analyst: *"The software showed it in green."*
Inspector: *"Why did you trust that?"*
Analyst: *"Because it's validated and I passed the LMS module."*

At that moment, your fancy AI tool becomes irrelevant because the human demonstrated no ownership of the rationale. Inspectors interpret that as:

- Potential data integrity risk
- Inadequate training program (21 CFR 211.25, EU GMP Ch. 2 §2.9)
- System reliance without human verification

One weak exchange can snowball into a Form 483 observation or a critical deficiency. The root cause is rarely malevolent intent. It is cognitive under-investment. People were trained where to click, not why they click.

3. Why Traditional Approaches Fail Under AI Pressure

Legacy training models struggle for four structural reasons:

1. **Static Content vs Dynamic Systems**
   GMP slide decks age slowly; AI decision rules evolve weekly. By the time your LMS refresher is due, the model behind your deviation triage engine has already been retrained twice.
2. **Procedural Recall vs Contextual Reasoning**
   Multiple-choice quizzes check memory of SOP numbers, not ability to reason when predictions and SOPs diverge.
3. **Monolithic Courses vs Micro-Adjustments**
   AI adoption creates micro-shifts in workflows: thresholds, alert frequencies, or validation reports. Traditional training is too infrequent and too broad.
4. **Individual Silos vs Cross-Disciplinary Cognition**
   AI outputs blend data from manufacturing, quality, maintenance, and supply chain. Analysts trained in narrow verticals cannot contextualize cross-signals.
5. Result: people follow system prompts until those prompts become ambiguous. In that ambiguity—where audits concentrate—training gaps reveal themselves.

4. The Cognitive Gap: Soft Skills Meet System Skills

Auditors increasingly evaluate whether personnel can:

- Explain underlying principles (pharmacopoeial, statistical, or risk-based) that drove the AI ruleset
- Recognize when the system might be wrong or incompletely configured
- Escalate anomalies even when no discrete alarm triggers

Achieving that capability requires two intertwined skill sets:

1. **System Literacy** – Knowing data flows, algorithm boundaries, and validation constraints
2. **Critical Reasoning** – Challenging assumptions, triangulating evidence, articulating risk
3. System literacy without reasoning leads to blind trust. Reasoning without literacy leads to speculation. Only their combination forms *audit-ready cognition.*

5. Principles of Effective AI-Era Training

Let us re-engineer the learning blueprint around five principles:

1. **Principle 1 – Learning as Risk Mitigation**
   Treat training as a *preventive control* in your Quality Risk Management (ICH Q9) framework, not as an HR requirement.
2. **Principle 2 – Contextual Anchoring**
   Anchor training scenarios in the actual data streams users see daily—batch release dashboards, deviation prioritization screens, or e-logbook entries.
3. **Principle 3 – Progressive Autonomy**
   Design curricula where users graduate through tiers

of independence: from guided actions to self-initiated challenges of the AI output.

4. **Principle 4 – Feedback Loops**
   Capture user insights and feed them back into both the algorithm retraining process and the training curriculum. Humans refine the model; the model informs humans.
5. **Principle 5 – Cognitive Diversity**
   Blend statisticians, operators, quality reviewers, and maintenance engineers in the same simulations. Cross-pollination prevents the "narrow lens" effect auditors often criticize.

6. The Four Levels of Audit-Conscious Thinking

Based on dozens of audit debriefs and CAPA workshops, I classify personnel cognition into four levels:

1. **Level 0 – Reactive**
   "I wait for alarms." Individuals rely entirely on system warnings.
2. **Level 1 – Procedural**
   "I follow the SOP step-by-step." Some awareness of regulation but limited adaptive capacity.
3. **Level 2 – Contextual**
   "I understand why the rule exists and can relate it to current data trends." Able to detect subtle misalignments.
4. **Level 3 – Anticipatory**
   "I foresee emerging risks, question system logic, and escalate before parameters drift." This is the inspector's benchmark for a *mature quality culture* (see PIC/S PI 041).

5. Your mission: elevate at least 70 % of frontline users to Level 2 and key decision-makers to Level 3. Technology alone cannot perform that lift.

7. Embedding AI Literacy Without Turning Everyone into Data Scientists

Many managers overcorrect and insist that every QC analyst learn Python or machine-learning theory. That is unnecessary and unrealistic. Instead, focus on four digestible competencies:

1. **Data Provenance** – Where did the numbers originate? What transformations occurred?
2. **Model Intention** – What business question does this AI component answer?
3. **Boundary Conditions** – Under which scenarios is the prediction unreliable?
4. **Human Override Protocol** – What is the documented mechanism to challenge or bypass the system?
5. An analyst who can fluently discuss those four points during an inspection will satisfy 90 % of the questioning, without writing a single line of code.

8. The DECIDE Framework—A Practical Cognitive Workflow

I teach a six-step mental checklist that fits seamlessly into GMP routines. You can incorporate it into SOPs or on-the-job coaching:

D – **Describe** the AI recommendation in plain language.
E – **Evaluate** supporting evidence (data set, timestamp, model version).

C – **Correlate** with process context (batch stage, environmental trends).
I – **Interpret** risk impact (quality, safety, supply).
D – **Decide** action (accept, adjust parameters, escalate).
E – **Explain** rationale in the electronic log (traceable knowledge).

DECIDE turns opaque algorithms into structured human reasoning that auditors can follow. It also reinforces data integrity by ensuring each conclusion is reproducible.

9. A Day in the Life—QC Analyst with an AI Assistant

Let us walk through one realistic scenario.

08:05 a.m. The LIMS dashboard flags *Sample 19-A* as "statistically atypical" in potency assay.
DECIDE in action:

- **Describe** – The system predicts a 5 % probability that the result belongs to the clean population.
- **Evaluate** – Check that data were captured via CDS with electronic signatures; review model version 3.2 introduced last week.
- **Correlate** – Look at parallel stability data; no trend deviations.
- **Interpret** – Potential OOS candidate; if confirmed, may delay batch release.
- **Decide** – Initiate "OOS-Screen" workflow, schedule confirmatory test.
- **Explain** – Enter comment: "Model 3.2 low confidence, manual review triggered per QC-SOP-481."

During audit, the inspector sees a clear rational chain, not just a red or green flag. The analyst owns the decision, while the AI accelerated detection.

10. Cross-Functional Mock Audits Using AI Simulations

One of the fastest ways to uplift cognition is to stage simulated regulatory inspections. Here is a tried-and-tested structure:

- **Preparation** – Extract anonymized historical data sets with embedded anomalies.
- **Roles** – Assign participants to inspector, SME, scribe, and system. Rotate roles each session.
- **Execution** – The "inspector" interrogates not only SOPs but the AI logic behind outlier detection, deviation triage, or predictive maintenance.
- **Debrief** – Capture where participants hesitated. Map those to training gaps, not individual blame.

Repeat quarterly; competence improves measurably, and real audits feel anticlimactic—a good sign.

11. Building a Culture of Challenge and Curiosity

Regulators increasingly associate maturity with the *ability to question systems without fear*. Encourage it through:

- **Psychological Safety** – Publicly commend staff who identified false positives or false negatives.
- **Transparent Metrics** – Share model performance dashboards with frontline teams, not just management.

- **Failure Forums** – Host monthly "model miss" meetings; dissect why a prediction failed and how humans caught it.

When curiosity is normalized, DECIDE becomes second nature, and inspectors feel that energy within minutes on the shop floor.

12. Common Pitfalls to Avoid

While upgrading training, several traps recur:

- **Dumping Tech Jargon** – Overwhelming employees with terms like "hyperparameter" erodes confidence.
- **One-Time Launch, No Refresh** – AI systems evolve; training must iterate.
- **Token Cross-Functional Sessions** – Superficial mixing of departments without real data leads to boredom and cynicism.
- **Ignoring Middle Management** – They translate strategy into daily coaching. If skipped, the initiative stalls.
- **Over-Automating Assessments** – AI-graded quizzes may test memory, not reasoning. Include live scenario discussions.

13. Measuring Training Effectiveness—Leading vs Lagging Indicators

Stop relying solely on lagging metrics such as "% curriculum completed." Introduce leading indicators that predict audit resilience:

- Frequency of human overrides per user
- Average time from AI alert to human action
- Number of models decommissioned due to user-reported concerns

- Cross-department attendance in simulation drills

When those metrics trend positively, you can expect smoother real-world inspections.

14. Regulatory Expectations on Training Records in the AI Era

Annex 11 and 21 CFR Part 11 already require evidence of "adequate training" for computerized systems. The AI layer intensifies scrutiny:

- **Traceability** – Link each user's training module version to the AI model version they interact with.
- **Competence Certification** – Record scenario-based assessments, not just course completions.
- **hange Control Integration** – Whenever model parameters change, trigger automatic evaluation of whether refresher training is needed.

Present these records proactively during an inspection; it signals mastery, not defensiveness.

15. Case Study—Biologics Plant that Rewired Its Training Approach

A 250-person facility producing monoclonal antibodies faced a close call when an FDA investigator challenged an analyst's understanding of an AI-driven media-fill monitoring system. The plant escaped with a minor observation but used the experience to revamp training:

1. Mapped all AI touchpoints across production, QC, and maintenance.
2. Introduced DECIDE as a universal cognitive language.

3. Set up monthly mock audits with an external retired inspector.
4. Integrated LMS with change control so that model retrains trigger micro-modules.
5. Within nine months, human overrides increased 40 % (showing healthy skepticism) while false escalations dropped. Their next MHRA inspection praised the "empowered staff capable of articulating system boundaries."

16. Key Takeaways

- Training is no longer a paperwork obligation; it is a frontline preventive control against data-integrity observations.
- Traditional click-through modules build record density, not cognitive depth.
- Effective AI-era training balances system literacy and critical reasoning.
- The DECIDE framework converts opaque predictions into auditable decisions.
- Cross-functional simulations and leading indicators are indispensable for continuous improvement.
- Regulators now expect traceable links between model updates and competency refreshers.

Bridging to the Next Chapter

You now have the architecture for transforming workforce compliance from passive acceptance into active, explainable judgment. In the next chapter we will zoom out from individual skills to the collective "Audit-Proof Mindset": the cultural operating system where technology, process, and human cognition converge into routine excellence—so robust that audits feel almost boring. Let us explore how to institutionalize that mindset across your entire organization.

Chapter 15

Training People to Think, Not Just Click

A Brief Look Back—and Forward

In the last chapter we focused on the technical side of winning regulator trust: architecture choices, validation approaches, and documentation patterns that make an AI-enabled system "audit speak." Yet no matter how immaculate the system design, a single distracted operator, an over-confident reviewer, or a bored manager can undo months of engineering in a moment.

Our next stop, therefore, is the human layer. If Part 5 is about building an audit-proof organization, the critical load-bearing wall is a workforce that can think—analytically, ethically, and situationally—while interacting with intelligent automation. After we finish here, the following chapter will explore the broader cultural posture—"The Audit-Proof Mindset." But first we must make sure people can execute that mindset competently, day in and day out.

1. Why "Click Training" Took Over Pharma

Walk into any manufacturing site on the Tuesday before an internal audit and you will hear a predictable chorus:

- "I just need every operator to click through the refresher modules."
- "Compliance means 100 % training completion—no exceptions."

- "If the LMS says they're trained, the inspector can't touch us."

That refrain is the product of two decades of well-intentioned evolution that drifted off course.

1. Computer-Based Training (CBT) solved a logistical nightmare. Once learning management systems (LMS) matured around 2005, the burden of instructor-led classes dropped sharply. Worksheets turned into quizzes; attendance rosters morphed into electronic signatures. Efficiency rose, and so did corporate enthusiasm.
2. Regulators appeared to endorse the shift—at least indirectly. Code of Federal Regulations 21 CFR 211 and EU Annex 15 demand documented evidence of training. An LMS printout is clean, timestamped, and, most importantly, easy to present.
3. KPI culture sealed the deal. When senior management asks, "How do we know our workforce is ready?" an LMS dashboard with green bars at 100 % is irresistible. It provides instant confidence—often illusory.
4. The unspoken side effect is cognitive atrophy. Employees learn that the organizational priority is a certificate of completion, not the substance or application of knowledge. The phrase "click next" becomes synonymous with training.

2. The Unseen Risk: Procedural Compliance Without Cognitive Engagement

If you sit across from an inspector long enough, a pattern emerges: the worst observations don't stem from ignorance of procedures. They originate in moments when procedures collide with reality and no one notices.

A simple example:

- An operator scans a barcode on a weighing balance; the MES flashes a non-blocking warning: "Calibration due in 2 days."
- The SOP says to stop if any calibration grace period is less than three days, but production targets are tight.
- The operator clicks "Acknowledge" and proceeds.

Four months later an OOS investigation reveals spiking variability in the product assay. The root cause analysis traces back to the same balance operating 48 hours past calibration. On paper the operator was fully trained—LMS shows 100 %. In reality, humans kept clicking.

Why it turns into a 483:

- Data integrity—The audit trail shows the warning was acknowledged, proving the system worked.
- Procedural failure—The operator overrode the SOP.
- Training gap—The site leaned on completion records rather than demonstrated understanding.

Inspectors see a paradox: technology flagging a risk that people actively ignore. The immediate question becomes, "What else is your staff ignoring?"

3. Cognitive Compliance: What Inspectors Look For

A seasoned inspector rarely opens a CAPA just because an individual made a mistake. They open it when the system fails to equip the individual with sufficient knowledge, time, or authority to act correctly. In an AI-enabled plant, that principle magnifies.

When regulators tour a line supported by predictive analytics or computer-vision checks, they probe three human-facing themes:

1. Decision Awareness
   • Can operators articulate why the AI recommendation is safe to follow—or to reject?
   • Do they recognize when a prediction falls outside the validated domain?
2. Procedural Context
   • Are SOPs updated to define how AI outputs map to actions?
   • Is there a clearly documented escalation path when the algorithm and human judgment disagree?
3. Continuous Learning
   • Does the organization systematically capture feedback to refine both the model and the procedure?
   • Are personnel trained to feed edge cases back into the lifecycle rather than silently override them?
4. In short, inspectors want evidence that humans are driving the system, not chauffeured by it.

4. Skill Sets for the AI-Enabled Quality Professional

Traditional GMP curricula emphasize process knowledge, documentation discipline, and an instinct for criticality. Those remain foundational. AI, however, adds a new layer of literacy that is conceptual rather than technical:

- Data Awareness
  Understand what "good data" look like, typical sources of bias, and why context matters.
- Model Scope Recognition
  Be able to state—in plain language—the intended use of the algorithm, its validated range, and known limitations.

- Risk Interpretation
  Translate a probability score or confidence interval into operational risk (e.g., "a 15 % false-negative rate means one missed contamination per eight batches at current volume").
- Decision Autonomy
  Know when human override is mandatory versus optional.
- Human-System Collaboration
  Maintain situational humility: the algorithm may catch what you miss, but you may perceive contextual cues the algorithm cannot. Alignment is a dialogue, not a vote.

These competencies sit somewhere between classical statistics and practical problem-solving. They do not require Python skills. They do demand structured thinking and a willingness to interrogate outputs rather than consume them passively.

5. Designing Training That Builds Judgment

Let us dissect how to design programs that foster thinking instead of rote clicking.

Step 1: Define Observable Behaviors
• "Can recognize when an algorithm is extrapolating beyond its training data"
• "Can articulate the rationale for rejecting or accepting an AI suggestion"
• "Initiates deviation filing when model misprediction impacts GxP outcome"

Step 2: Create Context-Rich Scenarios
Replace multiple-choice tests with micro-case studies. Example: present a deviation record containing sensor anomalies, then ask

the learner to decide whether the predictive maintenance alert constitutes a critical deviation or an informational note.

Step 3: Layer in Consequences
Simulate audit trails. If the learner ignores a safety warning, show downstream effects—batch rejection, patient risk, reputational damage. Adult learners internalize far better when they see the stakes.

Step 4: Enable Peer Debate
Incorporate group discussions where pairs defend opposing actions. The moderator highlights the alignment (or misalignment) with SOPs and risk principles. This bolsters critical thinking and reduces blind obedience to authority, including algorithmic authority.

Step 5: Close With Reflective Documentation
After each session, instruct participants to record:

- What they assumed
- What they discovered
- How their decision might change next time

The record becomes living evidence for auditors that your site's training emphasizes cognition, not checkboxes. More importantly, it sharpens personal metacognition—the ability to stand outside one's own thought process and evaluate it.

6. Embedding Critical Thinking Into Daily GxP Tasks

A common pushback is, "We can't hold a workshop every week. Production must continue." Agreed. The solution is to embed critical prompts inside workflow tools.

Example: During electronic batch record review, insert a mandatory free-text field: "Explain why any algorithmic risk score above 0.4 was accepted." The reviewer cannot finalize the record without typing a justification. The requirement halts "rubber-stamping" and creates an audit trail of rationale.

Another approach: Configure the QMS to route deviations flagged by AI through a dual review—one reviewer who trusts the prediction, another who questions it. The system pairs them randomly, forcing dialogue.

Over time, these micro-frictions cultivate a culture where thinking is habitual rather than exceptional.

7. Simulation-Based Learning: A Practical Blueprint

Pharma has borrowed simulation from aviation for years—think aseptic gowning drills or sterility test media simulations. AI introduces new dimensions worth simulating:

1. Data Drift Scenarios
   • Feed the model atypical input ranges and observe performance.
   • Learners must decide whether to continue, retrain, or shut down the system.
2. Adversarial Input
   • Introduce corrupted or malicious data to test cybersecurity awareness.
   • See how quickly staff detect "something feels off" even if metrics look normal.
3. Accountability Chain
   • Role-play an FDA inspection where the investigator questions model governance.
   • Participants practice explaining lifecycle documents, change control, and validation evidence.
4. Implementing simulation sounds resource-intensive, but it scales. A single scripted dataset and scenario tree can serve

multiple production lines with minor tweaks. The investment pales against the cost of a single major observation—let alone a consent decree.

8. Metrics That Matter: Measuring Thinking, Not Just Completion

Training metrics fall into three categories:

1. Activity Metrics—e.g., number of modules completed. Easy to capture, weak on insight.
2. Outcome Metrics—e.g., reduction in repeat deviations linked to human error. Influenced by many variables, but harder to ignore.
3. Cognitive Metrics—e.g., percentage of employees who can correctly outline model limits without aids. Requires spot audits, interviews, or real-time quizzes.
4. Moving from 1 to 3 is essential if you want to prove to both management and regulators that your teams are thinking.

Useful frameworks:

- "Cold Call" Interviews
  Quality leaders conduct random five-minute interviews on the floor. Questions: "What does this alarm mean? When would you escalate?" Responses logged anonymously for trend analysis.
- Shadow Audits
  Internal auditors accompany operators for a shift, noting not just actions but thought processes vocalized during tasks.
- Decision Sampling
  Analyze a subset of electronic records where AI

recommendations were overridden. Has the frequency and justification quality improved post-training?

When reporting upward, mix quantitative trends (e.g., 40 % reduction in unexplained overrides) with qualitative insights (e.g., "Operators now propose preventive actions unprompted").

9. Overcoming Resistance: From Fear of Automation to Ownership

Even seasoned professionals can feel threatened by AI. Fear manifests as two opposite behaviors: blind trust ("the system knows better than me, so I'll just follow it") and active sabotage ("this tech will replace me, so I'll prove it fails"). Both are audit liabilities.

Psychological levers to bridge the gap:

- Demystify
  Host "white-box" sessions where data scientists walk through model logic at a conceptual level.
- Personal Relevance
  Show how algorithmic insights lighten cognitive load—fewer repetitive checks, faster root cause analysis.
- Shared Credit
  When an early-warning model prevents downtime, celebrate both the engineering team and the line staff who acted on the alert. Ownership grows when recognition is shared.
- Safe Failure
  Use sandbox environments where experiments can fail without consequences. People gain confidence to question outputs.

Senior leadership must also signal, through policy, that human oversight remains paramount. Performance evaluations should reward discretionary thinking, not just system adherence.

10. Sustaining a Learning Culture in a High-Pressure Environment

Daily production pressures often squeeze training to the margins. Prevent that squeeze by integrating learning into existing rhythms:

- Shift Handover Rituals
  Add a two-minute "AI anomaly recap." Outgoing operators share any odd model behaviors with incoming staff, creating continuous informal training.
- Weekly CAPA Reviews
  Dedicate a slot for "algorithmic CAPAs." Discuss whether a human misinterpretation or a model misprediction was root cause, or both, and identify lessons.
- Quarterly Validation Refresh
  Incorporate line-level employees in retrospective analysis. Ask: "Did our risk assessments match real-world events? If not, should the next validation update adjust thresholds?"

Establishing these micro-events keeps knowledge fresh and situates learning inside operational context rather than as an extracurricular burden.

11. Common Pitfalls to Avoid

1. Confusing Familiarity With Competence
   A veteran operator may feel at home with the interface but still misinterpret confidence intervals.

2. Over-Abstracting AI
   Presenting AI as mystical breeds dependence or disdain. Stick to plain-language explanations anchored in process reality.
3. Training by Announcement
   Sending an email that "AI is now live" without a phased onboarding plan no longer passes regulatory muster.
4. Neglecting Supervisors
   Middle managers are a hidden failure mode. If they don't grasp the rationale behind algorithmic recommendations, they may override or dismiss them, erasing gains.
5. One-Size-Fits-All Modules
   A microbiologist and a data scientist need different depth. Tailor content or risk dilution.
6. Chasing the Shiny Thing
   Training budgets can vanish into trendy VR headsets rather than robust scenario design. Focus on cognitive outcomes, not gadgets.

12. Mindset Framework: Observe—Question—Explain—Decide (OQED)

To crystallize thinking habits, I use a four-step mental loop with teams. It works regardless of role or technology.

1. Observe
   • Notice what the system shows, what process data corroborate, what environmental cues exist.
   • Gather without judging.
2. Question
   • Ask, "Why might the algorithm be right? Why might it be wrong?"

• Check assumptions: data freshness, sensor integrity, unusual batch attributes.

3. Explain
   • Formulate a concise rationale you could defend to an inspector.
   • If you can't verbalize the reasoning, dig deeper.
4. Decide
   • Act—accept, override, or escalate.
   • Document the thought process so future reviewers and auditors see transparency.
5. OQED fits on a pocket card but rewires default behavior from clicking "Next" to thoughtful engagement. Encourage supervisors to use it during coaching moments. Over weeks, it becomes second nature and generates precisely the audit trail of reasoning regulators admire.

13. Key Takeaways

- Training completion metrics impress dashboards, not inspectors. Demonstrated judgment does.
- AI introduces new literacy requirements: data awareness, model scope recognition, risk interpretation, and human-system collaboration.
- Effective programs pivot around context-rich scenarios, consequence mapping, peer debate, and reflective documentation.
- Embedding critical prompts directly into routine tasks converts sporadic training into continuous thinking.
- Resistance dissipates when staff see personal relevance, shared credit, and safe environments to question algorithms.

- Sustaining learning in high-pressure environments relies on micro-rituals—shift handovers, CAPA reviews, validation refreshes.
- The OQED framework provides a portable mental model to operationalize cognitive compliance.

With people trained to think, not just click, the organization is structurally prepared to turn AI from a shiny project into a trusted co-worker. In the next chapter we'll widen the lens, exploring how to weave these individual competencies into a collective "Audit-Proof Mindset" that shapes policy, leadership, and everyday culture.

Chapter 16

Training People to Think, Not Just Click

A Quick Look Back

In the previous chapter we explored how to make AI regulator-friendly—architecting data flows, validation approaches, and governance models that keep inspectors nodding instead of frowning. That discussion inevitably raised a bigger question that every audit team, every senior manager, and certainly every inspector will ask:

"If the algorithm can guide decisions, do the people still understand what they're doing?"

This chapter exists to answer that question—and to give you a playbook for ensuring the answer is always an unqualified "yes."

1. The Illusion of "System-Trained" Personnel

Walk through any modern plant and you will hear a reassuring phrase: "We trained everyone on the new system."

On the surface the statement feels solid. There are sign-in sheets, e-learning completion reports, and maybe even an exam result. But probe a little deeper:

- Ask the operator to explain **why** the system flags a particular pH reading as critical.
- Ask the quality associate to tell you what data-integrity risk level is assigned to an unreviewed chromatogram.

- Ask the maintenance engineer to articulate the rationale behind the 24-hour re-qualification window the equipment health module recommends.

Too often you'll be met with a polite shrug.

The individual knows **where** to click, not **why** the click matters.

That is the illusion of system-trained personnel. It is comforting until an inspector starts asking open-ended questions—and then it unravels quickly.

2. Clicking Through SOPs: The Uncomfortable Reality

To understand how we got here, let's retrace a typical training path:

1. New digital or AI-assisted system gets implemented.
2. Vendor supplies templated SOPs, quick-start guides, and a short slide deck.
3. QA converts those materials into a standard training package.
4. Employees sit through a 60-minute Webex or classroom session.
5. An online quiz—10 multiple-choice items—confirms "competence."
6. Certificates are filed. Audit readiness box ticked.
7. The uncomfortable reality is that this workflow checks *documentation* boxes but rarely touches *cognitive* ones. People remember surface navigation because that is what is demonstrated. They have no mental models for risk, failure modes, or regulatory principles embedded in the technology.

When an inspector asks:

"Describe the algorithm's decision logic that determines extended sampling intervals,"

—silence.

Because the training never demanded that depth of understanding.

3. The Cognitive Gap Inspectors Spot in Minutes

Experienced regulators are exceptional at finding the seam between rote compliance and real comprehension. They use four simple probes:

- "Walk me through your last deviation—what failed in the thinking process?"
- "Why is step 37 required if the software already verifies dose weight?"
- "How would you know if the AI model starts drifting?"
- "Under what circumstances would you override the system's recommendation?"

If answers circle back to phrases like "the SOP says so" or "the system alerted me," the inspector notes a red flag: **process without principle.** In a data-driven era, that deficiency maps directly onto 483 observations under sub-parts dealing with *training*, *data integrity*, and *quality oversight*.

4. Why Traditional Training Programs Stagnate

Traditional GMP training was never designed for adaptive systems. Its most common weaknesses:

1. **Static Content:** PowerPoint decks freeze knowledge at implementation day. AI models, by definition, evolve.

2. **One-Size-Fits-All:** Operators, analysts, and supervisors receive identical material even though their cognitive loads differ.
3. **Testing for Recall, Not Reasoning:** Multiple-choice quizzes reward memory of button locations, not risk-based judgment.
4. **Audit-Centric Scheduling:** Training bursts occur before a re-inspection, not as part of daily work.
5. **Minimal Feedback Loop:** Post-training performance data rarely feeds back into content improvement.
6. In the age of algorithmic assistance these limitations are magnified. The system improves itself; the people remain frozen in yesterday's mental model—a fatal divergence.

5. Thinking Frameworks vs. Button Paths

A quality-driven organization does not train people *how to navigate* a system; it trains them *how to interrogate* one. I use a simple distinction when assessing readiness:

- **Button Path:** "Click Menu → Batch → QA Release → Generate Report."
- **Thinking Framework:** "First validate the data lineage for completeness, then challenge outlier detection rules, finally confirm release criteria alignment with the filing."

An operator fluent in button paths can function on a good day. An operator armed with a thinking framework can recover on a bad one. Audits are designed around bad days.

6. Where AI Becomes a Silent Coach

Ironically, the same AI that risks numbing critical thinking can be configured to sharpen it—if we design for that objective. There are three practical avenues:

1. **Contextual Prompts**
   Instead of auto-advancing through forms, the interface surfaces a brief "Why this matters" note each time critical parameters are entered. Over time, pattern recognition reinforces cognitive links.
2. **Socratic Hints**
   When a user tries to accept a dubious trend, the system can ask, "Which failure mode does this trend align with in your FMEA?" This nudges reflection without halting workflow.
3. **Post-Action Debrief**
   After completing a complex task, the software provides a mini-dashboard: performance indicators, compliance checkpoints missed, and recommended short reads. The feedback loop is immediate, personalized, and embedded into actual work—far more effective than yearly GMP refreshers.

7. Designing a Risk-Literate Workforce

Risk literacy is the skill that enables employees to challenge AI suggestions intelligently. To cultivate it, I use the **"Three Layers"** approach:

1. **Regulatory Layer** – Teach the governing principle (e.g., ALCOA+ for data integrity).
2. **Process Layer** – Map how that principle manifests in the specific workflow (e.g., audit trail review frequency).

3. **Algorithm Layer** – Explain how the AI enforces or monitors the principle (e.g., anomaly detection on time-stamped edits).
4. People who grasp all three layers can mentally triangulate any exception. They understand *why*, *where*, and *how* simultaneously. That becomes evident to auditors—in a good way.

8. Continual Learning Loops: From Shift Log to Neural Net

Annual classroom training is incompatible with adaptive manufacturing. Instead we integrate "learning moments" into operational signals:

- **Shift Huddles:** Present yesterday's most interesting false positive flagged by the AI. Debate root cause for five minutes.
- **Deviation Trending Meetings:** Invite the algorithm to predict which step will generate the next class-2 deviation. Challenge the logic; refine it on the spot.
- **Cross-Functional Clinics:** Every fortnight, one department showcases how AI informed their decision. Peers critique and extrapolate to their own areas.

Notice what is missing? Slides. Quizzes. Click fatigue. Learning is now a behavioral loop nested inside production rhythms.

9. Mistakes to Avoid When Rolling Out AI-Enabled Training

Even well-meaning programs stumble. Watch out for these common pitfalls:

- **Over-Gamification:** Leaderboards can turn learning into points chasing rather than risk understanding.
- **Blind Trust in Chatbots:** A GPT-style assistant that fetches SOP snippets but never links back to regulatory clauses can propagate partial truths.
- **Ignoring Cognitive Load:** Flashy dashboards might overwhelm shop-floor personnel already juggling alarms, PPE adjustments, and throughput targets.
- **One-Off Workshops:** A spectacular launch event followed by silence breeds cynicism faster than no training at all.
- **Shadow IT Fixes:** When official content lags, teams build unofficial cheat sheets—a data-integrity threat in disguise.

10. The "Ask Why Twice" Model—A Practical Framework

After a decade of rescuing audit findings linked to training, I distilled a minimalist yet powerful model:

1. **First Why: Regulatory Anchor**
   "Why does the regulation care about this parameter?" Forces the learner to name the clause, guideline, or principle.
2. **Second Why: Risk Expression**
   "Why does a loss of control here create patient or product risk?" Connects the abstract rule to tangible harm.
3. A session—or system prompt—is incomplete until both whys are answered. The model is nimble; it can run in a 30-second AI chatbot interaction, a five-minute huddle, or a one-hour root-cause deep-dive.

11. Case Study: A Batch Record Near-Miss Averted

Let's ground the theory in a real scenario (names and data altered):

Background: A biologics facility introduced an AI module that predicts fill-weight drift. Operators received standard navigation training, nothing more.

Event: During a campaign, the AI flagged a potential drift at 0.8σ—well below the deviation threshold. The system recommended "Monitor." The operator clicked "Acknowledge" without comment.

Inspection Day: Six weeks later, an MHRA inspector asked the operator, "What does 0.8σ mean in this context?" The operator shrugged. Red flag. The inspector escalated to QA.

Intervention: QA discovered 12 similar low-grade alerts with no justification notes. Potential latent deviation.

Fix:

1. Immediate corrective action—batch record addendum explaining statistical rationale.
2. Training redesign based on the **Ask Why Twice** model.
3. Interface update that forces a short free-text rationale for any alert acknowledgment above 0.5σ.
4. Weekly huddle review of all "monitor" clicks with the production team.
5. Outcome: Follow-up inspection six months later praised the facility for "clear operator understanding of statistical signals and documented scientific rationale." Near-miss converted into positive citation.

The hidden lesson: Teaching people *why* 0.8σ matters turned a blind click into a thoughtful decision, eliminating a potential 483.

12. From Compliance Anxiety to Situational Awareness

When training shifts from button paths to thinking frameworks, two cultural transformations emerge:

- **Reduced Fear of Judgment:** Employees speak openly about uncertainties because reflection is normalized.
- **Proactive Ownership:** Teams fine-tune AI thresholds, suggest new data features, and flag model drift before formal review cycles. They are no longer passengers but co-pilots.

Auditors read this energy instantly. They hear operators forecasting process hazards unprompted, and they know the quality system is alive.

13. Key Takeaways

- **System navigation is necessary but insufficient;** inspectors probe for reasoning, not rote clicks.
- Traditional training fails because it is static, recall-based, and event-driven.
- AI, if configured as a silent coach, can reinforce critical thinking through contextual prompts, Socratic hints, and post-action debriefs.
- Building risk literacy requires layering regulatory principles, process specifics, and algorithm logic.
- The minimalist **Ask Why Twice** model embeds reasoning in daily work without cognitive overload.
- Continual learning loops—shift huddles, deviation clinics, cross-functional showcases—keep training alive and adaptive.

- Avoid over-gamification, blind trust in chatbots, and one-off workshops; they erode credibility.
- An audit-proof organization is one where people understand *why* they click, not just *where* they click.

Transition to Next Chapter

Now that we have equipped your workforce to think critically in an AI-enabled environment, the natural next challenge is scaling that mindset across the entire organization—beyond SOP tweaks and into cultural DNA. In the following chapter, we will examine how to foster **The Audit-Proof Mindset**—a collective stance where anticipation replaces reaction and where both humans and algorithms play in symphony to make audits, well, almost boring.

Chapter 17

The Future of Audits Will Be Boring (And That's Good)

A Natural Lead-In

In Chapter 16 we explored "The Audit-Proof Mindset"—the habits, heuristics, and cultural signals that keep an organization calm under regulatory scrutiny. Now let's zoom out and ask a bigger question: *What happens when that mindset becomes the norm, assisted by mature AI and automation?*

The short answer is that audits will become uneventful. Inspectors will still arrive, standards will still apply, but the drama, the frantic document hunts, and the career-threatening surprises will fade into background noise. In other words, the future of audits is *boring*—and that is precisely the point.

1. Why "Boring" Is the Ultimate KPI

Most pharmaceutical KPIs track either output (batches released, deviations closed) or cost (OEE, yield). Rarely do we measure *adrenaline spikes*. Yet if you mapped heart-rates inside a plant during an unannounced FDA inspection, you would see them surge, then crash, then surge again as each finding unfolds.

A "boring" audit is one in which:

- Nobody runs to find boxes or back-up files.

- Personnel speak in measured tones because they actually know the process.
- Data retrieval is instantaneous, transparent, and context-complete.
- Inspectors spend more time acknowledging good practices than documenting deficiencies.

Boredom, here, is a proxy for *process fluency*. It signals that compliance is embedded so deeply that the distinction between "normal operations" and "audit mode" no longer exists.

2. From Firefighting to Flow

Most plants still oscillate between two states:

1. **Production Mode**—Ship product, meet demand, keep utilities humming.
2. **Audit Mode**—Freeze production lines, summon SMEs, print records, apply temporary patches.
3. The future plant will operate in a single state: **Flow Mode**. In Flow Mode, every activity—manufacturing, testing, deviations, change control—is *continuously* audit-ready, because the risk signals, data integrity checks, and cross-process reconciliations happen in real time. AI is not a special project; it is the silent supervisor that prevents chaos from accumulating in the first place.

3. The Emerging Regulatory Landscape

Regulators are under the same pressure as industry: to do more with less while safeguarding public health. Three quiet shifts are already shaping how future inspections will unfold.

- **Data-Centric Guidance**
  Both FDA's "Computer Software Assurance" draft guidance and EMA's Annex 11 revision emphasize data risk over documentation volume. Expect deeper sampling of raw data sets and metadata, not just review of paper printouts.
- **Remote and Hybrid Inspections**
  COVID-19 catalyzed remote assessments. The model persists because it works. By 2030, hybrid audits—part on-site, part remote, part continuous data sharing—will be routine.
- **Algorithmic Forensics**
  Inspectors now receive training in basic analytics. Tomorrow they will come armed with scriptable tools that ingest log files on the spot, search for timestamp anomalies, and flag suspicious patterns. Manual obfuscation tricks will be instantly exposed.

The takeaway: automation will not weaken oversight; it will sharpen it. Only systems designed for transparency, explainability, and traceability will thrive under such scrutiny.

4. AI as Invisible Infrastructure

If early AI deployments felt like bolt-on gadgets, mature implementations vanish into the wallpaper.

1. **Predictive Compliance Engines**
   Always-on models scan process control data, batch records, and stability trends, calculating compliance "delta scores." When a parameter drifts toward a spec boundary, users receive context-enriched alerts that include probable root causes and recommended preventive actions.

2. **Cognitive Data Fabric**
   Structured and unstructured content—chromatogram images, SOP revisions, audit trail logs—link through a semantic layer. The result: one search query retrieves every artifact tied to a lot number or equipment ID, complete with chain-of-custody confirmation.
3. **Self-Explaining Smart Forms**
   Instead of blank fields, forms teach while you fill them. If you enter a value inconsistent with a trend, the form pauses, cites the relevant SOP clause, and offers correct ranges. Compliance shifts left, at the data entry stage.
4. These capabilities are *unobtrusive.* Operators focus on science and quality, not on wrestling with software.

5. A Day in 2030: What an Audit Looks Like

Let's perform a quick time-travel exercise. Imagine you are the Quality Head in 2030.

08:30 AM—The inspector logs into the regulator portal one week before arrival and pre-screens your digital dashboards. Most KPIs show green. A single amber flag appears in the sterility suite microbiological monitoring trend.

09:15 AM—Your AI system automatically surfaces the micro-deviation report plus a video clip of the root-cause analysis conducted days earlier. The inspector sees risk mitigation already in place.

10:00 AM—On-site now, the inspector requests five random batch records. You tap a tablet. Within seconds, authenticated PDF renderings plus embedded sensor metadata load on a shared screen.

11:30 AM—They ask a production operator to explain a cleaning changeover. The worker opens an AR visor that displays the current, controlled SOP and shows the last three executed runs. He walks through each step; no coaching from supervisors needed.

12:45 PM—Over lunch, the inspector mentions that your deviation closure time is 48 % faster than industry median. You didn't know this KPI, but the system benchmarked it automatically.

03:00 PM—Final wrap-up. No Form 483. Just one recommendation: publish your risk-scoring algorithm so the agency can consider it in future guidance. You nod, secretly proud that your once "boring" operation now sets the standard.

6. Evolving Roles: From Documentation Clerks to Risk Strategists

The fear that "AI will take my job" dissipates when people experience how mind-numbing their old tasks were.

- **Document Coordinators**
  Transition into Information Curators, validating ontology rules and governing metadata lifecycles.
- **QC Analysts**
  Become Data Pattern Investigators, focusing on outlier interpretation rather than routine peak integration.
- **Validation Engineers**
  Shift from test-script writers to Model Governance Leads, defining parameters for algorithm performance, drift detection, and retraining cadence.
- **Line Operators**
  Evolve into Process Sentinels who interpret predictive dashboards, intervene early, and feed human context back into learning loops.

The skill mix moves toward *critical thinking*, *risk communication*, and *system ethics*. Paper pushing fades; decision quality rises.

7. New Metrics: Signal-to-Noise Ratio Over Paper Volume

Traditional compliance equated quantity with thoroughness. Think of the 5,000-page validation binder—impressive to look at, impossible to digest. The future replaces volume-based metrics with signal-based metrics:

- **Traceability Density**
  The proportion of data objects linked via contextual tags to their upstream and downstream impact points.
- **Prediction Fidelity**
  How accurately system early-warning models align with human SME assessments and eventual outcomes.
- **Cognitive Load Index**
  Time an average user needs to locate, understand, and act upon a compliance-critical data set.

Aim high on these metrics, and the inspection will take care of itself.

8. Ethical Guardrails in a Hyper-Automated World

When AI decisions invisibly shape plant behavior, ethical lapses can propagate at machine speed. Three guardrails will keep you safe:

1. **Algorithmic Transparency**
   Maintain clear documentation of model purpose, input data, training logic, validation results, and version history. Provide inspectors human-readable explanations, not just code dumps.
2. **Human-In-the-Loop Overrides**
   Even the most accurate model can misfire. Policies must empower users to challenge or bypass AI recommendations without fear of blame.

3. **Bias Surveillance**
   Continuously monitor for data drift that skews outputs—for example, a sensor type that under-reports during humidity spikes, or a training set over-weighted toward batch failures. Audit logs should capture both detected bias and corrective measures.
4. Ethics is not a side show; it is the new validation.

9. Common Illusions About the Future—And How to Avoid Them

1. **"The Regulator Will Never Catch Up."**
   Reality: Agencies are already piloting their own AI screeners. Assume parity or you will be outflanked.
2. **"Once the System Is Validated, We're Done."**
   Reality: Models drift. Continuous verification will replace one-and-done IQ/OQ/PQ mindsets.
3. **"Human Error Will Disappear."**
   Reality: Error types will change, not vanish. Expect more *interpretation errors* (misreading dashboards) instead of data entry typos.
4. **"Boring Means Easy."**
   Reality: Sustained boredom requires disciplined design, rigorous maintenance, and relentless vigilance.

10. Building Your Personal Roadmap Toward the Boring Audit

Step 1: **Map Current Pain Points**
Where do last-minute scrambles originate? Identify process choke points, tooling gaps, and skill deficits.

Step 2: **Define Boredom Indicators**
Imagine a future inspection. List behaviors that signal calm readiness—e.g., instant data retrieval, SME confidence, aligned narratives.

Step 3: **Prioritize Foundational Automations**
Start with rule-based bots that standardize document naming, time-stamp reconciliation, and cross-system indexing.

Step 4: **Layer Predictive Analytics**
Once data is clean and linked, deploy models that flag emerging risks. Validate small, scale carefully, document relentlessly.

Step 5: **Embed Cultural Reinforcement**
Reward teams for early detection, not heroic fixes. Celebrate uneventful audits as organizational victories, not non-events.

Step 6: **Iterate, Measure, and Share**
Publish internal metrics. Compare against industry benchmarks. Incorporate lessons into SOP updates. Boredom is not static; it must be maintained.

11. Closing Thoughts: A Final Conversation Between Future You and Today You

Picture yourself five years from now, walking an inspector through a facility where every screen, sensor, and employee radiates quiet assurance. Future You turns to Today You and says:

"I'm glad you treated AI as an enabler, not a miracle. I'm glad you invested in people, not just systems. Most of all, I'm glad you aimed for boredom. That single word forced us to strip away drama, expose hidden risks, and rebuild processes we could trust with our careers—and with patients' lives."

Today You nods. Because you now understand that a boring audit is not the absence of action; it is the culmination of thousands of micro-actions performed correctly, invisibly, every day.

12. Key Takeaways

- Strive for audits so uneventful they feel routine; boredom is a leading indicator of process maturity.
- Future regulators will use their own analytics; design systems for transparency and explainability now.
- AI's highest value lies in continuous, invisible risk sensing—not flashier, one-off automation.
- Organizational roles will shift toward risk strategy, model governance, and ethical oversight.
- New success metrics focus on signal quality and user cognitive load, not binder thickness.
- Ethical guardrails—transparency, overrides, bias monitoring—are as critical as validation protocols.
- A structured roadmap moves from pain-point mapping to cultural reinforcement; aim for incremental, validated gains.
- The boring audit is a promise kept to patients, regulators, and your own professional future.

The book ends here, but your work begins now. The next Form 483 that doesn't appear, the next audit that ends with a handshake instead of a warning letter—those quiet victories will be your proof that AI, applied wisely, turns fear into confidence and crisis into calm routine.

Chapter 18

Artificial Intelligence as an Enabler of Pharmaceutical Quality: Aligning Innovation with ICH Q10 and ICH Q11

Introduction: AI Does Not Replace the Quality System—It Reveals It

Artificial Intelligence is often discussed in the pharmaceutical industry as a disruptive technology, a productivity booster, or a digital transformation driver. Rarely is it discussed in the language that regulators actually use: **system effectiveness, process understanding, lifecycle management, and continual improvement**. This mismatch in language is one of the primary reasons why AI initiatives in pharmaceutical companies struggle to gain acceptance during audits or fail to deliver meaningful quality outcomes.

ICH Q10 (Pharmaceutical Quality System) and ICH Q11 (Development and Manufacture of Drug Substances) were never written with artificial intelligence in mind. Yet, when examined carefully, both guidelines are fundamentally aligned with the very strengths AI offers—**pattern recognition, knowledge integration, consistency, and proactive risk identification**. The challenge is not whether AI fits into ICH Q10 or Q11. The real challenge is whether organizations implement AI in a way that **strengthens these guidelines instead of bypassing them**.

This chapter explores how artificial intelligence, when applied responsibly, can act as a **quality enabler** rather than a compliance risk. It does not propose AI as a replacement for scientific judgment, pharmaceutical development principles, or quality oversight. Instead, it positions AI as a **supporting layer** that enhances the intent and execution of ICH Q10 and ICH Q11 across the product lifecycle.

1. Understanding the Intent of ICH Q10 Before Introducing AI

ICH Q10 establishes a comprehensive Pharmaceutical Quality System that spans the entire product lifecycle—from development through technology transfer, commercial manufacturing, and product discontinuation. Its core objective is not documentation compliance but **consistent product quality achieved through effective system design and management responsibility**.

At its heart, ICH Q10 is built on four key pillars:

1. **Process Performance and Product Quality Monitoring System**
2. **Corrective and Preventive Action (CAPA) System**
3. **Change Management System**
4. **Management Review of Process Performance and Product Quality**
5. These elements are supported by quality risk management (ICH Q9) and knowledge management principles. Importantly, ICH Q10 emphasizes **science- and risk-based decision-making**, continual improvement, and effective communication of quality knowledge.

Artificial intelligence, when mapped correctly, does not sit outside this structure. It operates **within these pillars**, primarily as a **knowledge amplification mechanism**. AI does not create quality; it makes existing quality signals more visible, connected, and actionable.

2. AI and Knowledge Management: The Missing Link in ICH Q10 Execution

ICH Q10 repeatedly emphasizes knowledge management as a critical enabler of the Pharmaceutical Quality System. However, in practice, knowledge in pharmaceutical organizations remains fragmented—stored across SOPs, validation reports, development studies, deviation records, and individual experience.

Artificial intelligence offers a structured way to **connect and analyze this fragmented knowledge** without altering its ownership or scientific basis. By identifying relationships between development data, manufacturing performance, deviations, and changes, AI supports the intent of ICH Q10 without redefining it.

For example, AI systems can:

- Identify recurring quality trends across batches that are not obvious through manual review
- Correlate deviations with specific process parameters or material attributes
- Highlight inconsistencies between development assumptions and commercial performance
- In this context, AI does not make decisions. It **surfaces insights** that allow quality professionals to make better, faster, and more consistent decisions—exactly what ICH Q10 expects from an effective quality system.

3. Process Performance and Product Quality Monitoring: From Reactive to Predictive

One of the most operationally demanding elements of ICH Q10 is the Process Performance and Product Quality Monitoring System. Traditionally, this system relies heavily on periodic reviews, trending reports, and manual statistical analysis. While effective to a degree, such approaches are often retrospective and limited by human capacity.

Artificial intelligence enhances this system by enabling:

- Continuous monitoring instead of periodic review
- Detection of subtle trends across multiple parameters
- Early identification of drift before specifications are breached
- This does not change the regulatory expectation. Specifications, acceptance criteria, and control strategies remain exactly as defined. What changes is the **timing and depth of visibility**. AI allows organizations to identify emerging risks earlier, supporting the proactive quality management philosophy embedded in ICH Q10.

From a regulatory perspective, this aligns strongly with the guideline's intent to maintain a **state of control**, not merely demonstrate it during inspections.

4. AI and CAPA Systems: Strengthening Root Cause Analysis, Not Replacing It

CAPA effectiveness is one of the most frequently cited weaknesses in regulatory inspections. Root cause analyses are often superficial, corrective actions are reactive, and preventive actions are poorly justified. These failures are rarely due to lack of procedures; they are due to limited system-wide visibility.

Artificial intelligence supports CAPA systems by:

- Identifying patterns across historical deviations and complaints
- Highlighting recurring failure modes across different products or processes

- Providing data-driven context to support root cause hypotheses
- It is critical to emphasize that AI does not determine root causes. Root cause analysis remains a **human responsibility grounded in scientific reasoning**. AI's role is to reduce bias, expand the dataset under consideration, and prevent repetitive CAPA cycles caused by incomplete analysis.

When implemented this way, AI strengthens CAPA effectiveness in full alignment with ICH Q10 expectations.

5. Change Management Under ICH Q10: AI as an Impact Visibility Tool

Change management failures often occur not because changes are uncontrolled, but because their **full impact is not understood**. ICH Q10 requires changes to be evaluated based on risk, scientific understanding, and potential impact on product quality.

Artificial intelligence enhances change management by enabling:

- Cross-functional impact mapping using historical change data
- Identification of downstream risks based on similar past changes
- Improved consistency in risk classification and justification
- This does not eliminate the need for quality review, approval workflows, or regulatory assessment. Instead, it improves the **quality of information available to decision-makers**, reducing reliance on subjective judgment alone.

From an audit standpoint, this improves transparency and traceability—two outcomes strongly favored by regulators.

6. Management Review: Turning Data into Meaningful Oversight

ICH Q10 assigns clear responsibility to senior management for ensuring the effectiveness of the Pharmaceutical Quality System. However, management reviews often suffer from information overload without insight.

Artificial intelligence supports management review by:

- Summarizing complex quality data into meaningful patterns
- Highlighting systemic risks rather than isolated events
- Supporting evidence-based strategic decisions
- This allows management to fulfill their ICH Q10 responsibilities more effectively, reinforcing accountability rather than diluting it.

7. ICH Q11: Scientific Understanding as the Foundation of AI Use

ICH Q11 focuses on the development and manufacture of drug substances, emphasizing scientific understanding, identification of critical quality attributes (CQAs), critical process parameters (CPPs), and lifecycle management.

A key principle of ICH Q11 is that **process understanding should be built during development and refined throughout the product lifecycle**. Artificial intelligence aligns naturally with this principle when used as a knowledge integration tool.

AI does not replace development studies, design of experiments, or mechanistic understanding. Instead, it:

- Integrates development data with commercial manufacturing experience

- Identifies long-term trends affecting CQAs
- Supports continual process verification
- In this way, AI becomes a **bridge between development knowledge and commercial reality**, strengthening the lifecycle approach required by ICH Q11.

8. AI and Control Strategy Optimization Under ICH Q11

ICH Q11 emphasizes the importance of a robust control strategy based on scientific understanding and risk management. Control strategies often evolve over time as more data becomes available, yet organizations struggle to utilize accumulated data effectively.

Artificial intelligence enables:

- Evaluation of control strategy effectiveness using real manufacturing data
- Identification of redundant or weak controls
- Data-driven refinement of monitoring approaches
- This does not imply automated control changes. Any modification remains subject to change control, regulatory assessment, and validation. AI's role is to **inform improvement**, not execute it.

9. Lifecycle Management: Where ICH Q10 and Q11 Truly Meet AI

The intersection of ICH Q10 and ICH Q11 lies in lifecycle management. Development knowledge must inform commercial manufacturing, and commercial experience must feed back into continual improvement.

Artificial intelligence strengthens this feedback loop by:

- Preserving development knowledge beyond individual contributors
- Preventing loss of process understanding over time
- Supporting consistent decision-making across product lifecycle stages
- This directly supports the regulatory expectation that quality systems mature rather than stagnate after approval.

10. Regulatory Acceptability: The Conditions Under Which AI Aligns with ICH

Regulatory acceptance of AI depends not on the technology itself but on **how it is governed**. From an ICH Q10 and Q11 perspective, AI systems must:

- Be risk-based in design and use
- Be transparent in purpose and limitations
- Support, not replace, human oversight
- Be validated proportionate to their impact on product quality
- When these conditions are met, AI does not conflict with ICH guidelines. Instead, it becomes an extension of their original intent.

11. The Human Role Remains Central

Both ICH Q10 and ICH Q11 are explicit about management responsibility, scientific judgment, and accountability. Artificial intelligence does not alter this responsibility. If anything, it increases it by making system weaknesses more visible.

Quality professionals remain responsible for:

- Interpreting AI outputs
- Making final decisions
- Ensuring ethical and compliant use
- AI is not a shield against regulatory action. It is a **mirror that reflects system maturity**.

12. Conclusion: AI as a Maturity Test of the Quality System

Artificial intelligence does not make a weak quality system stronger. It makes weaknesses clearer. In organizations with mature Pharmaceutical Quality Systems aligned with ICH Q10 and ICH Q11, AI becomes a powerful enabler of consistency, visibility, and continual improvement. In organizations without such maturity, AI exposes gaps rather than hiding them.

The true impact of AI in relation to ICH Q10 and Q11 is not technological. It is cultural. It reflects whether an organization truly understands its processes, manages risk proactively, and values knowledge over documentation volume.

Used correctly, AI does not change the rules of pharmaceutical quality.

It helps organizations finally play by them—consistently.

Chapter 19

Artificial Intelligence and Quality Risk Management During Pharmaceutical Audits

1. Introduction: Why Risk Management, Not AI, Decides Audit Outcomes

Pharmaceutical audits do not fail because organizations lack procedures. They fail because **risks are misunderstood, underestimated, or discovered too late**. Regulators do not expect zero risk; they expect **controlled, understood, and actively managed risk**. This distinction is fundamental to Quality Risk Management (QRM) as defined by ICH Q9 and reinforced through ICH Q10.

Artificial Intelligence has entered pharmaceutical operations at a time when regulatory expectations around risk management have matured significantly. Inspectors today are less interested in whether a company can recite definitions of risk assessment tools and more interested in whether the organization **recognizes emerging risks early, prioritizes them correctly, and responds proportionately**.

This chapter examines the relationship between Artificial Intelligence and Quality Risk Management specifically **in the context of pharmaceutical audits**. It does not position AI as a risk management system on its own, nor does it suggest that AI can replace established QRM methodologies such as FMEA, HACCP, or risk ranking and filtering. Instead, it explores how AI functions as a **risk visibility and consistency layer**, enhancing the effectiveness of existing QRM processes during audit preparation, execution, and follow-up.

2. The Regulator's View of Quality Risk Management During Audits

To understand where AI fits, one must first understand **how regulators evaluate Quality Risk Management during an audit**. Inspectors do not audit risk registers in isolation. They assess whether risk management is **embedded into daily decision-making**.

During audits, regulators typically look for:

- Evidence that risks are identified proactively, not only after deviations
- Logical linkage between risk assessments and actual controls
- Consistency between stated risks and observed practices
- Appropriate escalation of high-risk issues
- Effectiveness of risk-based decision-making over time
- A common audit finding is not "absence of risk management," but rather **superficial risk management**—risk assessments that exist on paper but are disconnected from operational reality. This is where artificial intelligence becomes relevant, not as a new regulatory requirement, but as a mechanism to **reduce subjectivity, bias, and fragmentation** in QRM execution.

3. The Structural Weaknesses of Traditional QRM in Pharma

Before discussing AI, it is important to acknowledge the inherent limitations of traditional Quality Risk Management approaches as practiced in many pharmaceutical organizations.

4. Fragmented Risk Ownership

Risks are often assessed within functional silos:

- Manufacturing risks assessed by production
- Quality risks assessed by QA
- Data integrity risks assessed by IT
- Regulatory risks assessed by RA
- Auditors, however, assess **systemic risk**, not functional risk. Artificial intelligence helps surface cross-functional patterns that are otherwise invisible.

5. Retrospective Risk Recognition

Many risk assessments are triggered only after:

- Deviations
- Audit observations
- Complaints
- Regulatory actions
- This reactive approach contradicts the preventive intent of QRM. AI shifts risk recognition **upstream**, identifying weak signals before formal failures occur.

6. Inconsistent Risk Scoring

Risk scoring often varies depending on:

- Who performs the assessment
- Time pressure
- Organizational bias
- Fear of escalation
- AI does not decide risk severity, but it highlights **inconsistencies and historical outcomes**, enabling more objective discussions.

7. Artificial Intelligence as a Risk Visibility Layer

Artificial intelligence should be understood as a **risk visibility layer**, not a risk authority. It aggregates, correlates, and analyzes data across systems that were never designed to communicate holistically.

During pharmaceutical audits, this visibility becomes critical because inspectors evaluate whether:

- Risks were foreseeable
- Signals were ignored or acted upon
- Decisions were proportionate to known risks
- AI supports this by:
- Identifying recurring low-level deviations that collectively indicate high risk
- Correlating audit observations with historical CAPAs and changes
- Highlighting risk drift over time rather than isolated events
- Importantly, AI does not redefine risk; it **reveals risk accumulation**.

8. Quality Risk Management Across Audit Phases

To fully understand the relationship between AI and QRM, it is useful to examine the audit lifecycle itself.

9. Pre-Audit Phase: Risk Anticipation

Before an audit begins, organizations typically perform:

- Internal audits
- Gap assessments
- Mock inspections
- These activities often rely on manual checklists and subjective judgment. AI enhances pre-audit QRM by:
- Identifying historical audit pain points
- Highlighting areas with repeated minor observations
- Detecting documentation-execution mismatches
- This allows organizations to prioritize **true audit risks**, not just visible deficiencies.

10. During the Audit: Risk Exposure Management

During audits, inspectors continuously assess:

- How the organization responds to questions
- Whether explanations align with documented risk assessments
- How deviations and risks are contextualized
- AI supports audit-time QRM indirectly by:
- Ensuring consistency in data presented
- Reducing last-minute data reconciliation errors

- Supporting confident, evidence-based responses
- While AI should not be actively "used" during audits in a visible manner, its preparatory role directly influences audit outcomes.

11. Post-Audit Phase: Risk-Based CAPA and Remediation

Post-audit remediation often fails because organizations treat observations as isolated findings rather than risk signals. AI supports post-audit QRM by:

- Mapping observations to underlying systemic risks
- Identifying similar latent risks not explicitly cited
- Supporting proportionate CAPA design
- This aligns strongly with regulatory expectations for **preventive rather than cosmetic CAPAs**.

12. AI and Risk Identification: Seeing What Humans Miss

Risk identification is the most critical and weakest element of QRM. Human risk identification is limited by:

- Cognitive bias
- Time constraints
- Data volume
- Artificial intelligence excels at identifying:
- Weak signals across large datasets
- Rare but recurring anomalies
- Correlations that do not fit existing mental models

- In the context of audits, this helps organizations identify:
- Emerging data integrity risks
- Process drift that remains within specifications
- Training effectiveness gaps masked by completion metrics
- This does not replace human judgment; it **challenges complacency**.

13. Risk Analysis and Evaluation: Supporting, Not Automating Decisions

Regulators remain clear that risk evaluation must involve **scientific judgment and quality oversight**. AI supports this process by:

- Providing historical outcome context
- Highlighting consequence patterns
- Identifying mismatches between risk ratings and actual impact
- For example, if low-risk changes consistently lead to deviations, AI highlights this inconsistency, prompting reassessment of risk criteria.

14. Risk Control: Making Controls Proportionate and Effective

One of the most common audit criticisms is **over-control**—excessive procedural layers that do not reduce risk but increase complexity. AI supports risk control by:

- Identifying ineffective controls
- Highlighting redundant reviews
- Supporting simplification without loss of control

- This is particularly relevant in audits where inspectors question why controls exist without clear risk justification.

15. Risk Communication and Documentation: Audit Transparency

Auditors do not expect perfect systems. They expect **clear reasoning**. AI supports risk communication by:

- Improving traceability of risk decisions
- Supporting consistent narratives across documents
- Reducing contradiction between different quality records
- This enhances audit credibility.

16. Governance of AI Within QRM

From a regulatory perspective, AI itself becomes a risk that must be managed. Organizations must:

- Define AI's role clearly
- Establish oversight mechanisms
- Validate AI use proportionate to impact
- Maintain human accountability
- When AI governance is weak, it becomes an audit liability rather than an asset.

17, Interim Reflection: AI Does Not Reduce Risk—It Reduces Blindness

At this stage, one principle becomes clear:
Artificial intelligence does not eliminate quality risk. It reduces the organization's blindness to it.

Auditors penalize blindness far more harshly than risk itself.

Artificial Intelligence and Quality Risk Management During Pharmaceutical Audits

PART 2—Risk Principles, ICH Q9 Alignment, and Audit Reality

18. Re-anchoring AI Within the Principles of ICH Q9

Any serious discussion of Quality Risk Management during pharmaceutical audits must be grounded in **ICH Q9**, because inspectors implicitly evaluate QRM maturity through this lens—even when they do not explicitly cite the guideline.

ICH Q9 is built on a few non-negotiable principles:

- Risk is a **combination of probability and severity**
- Risk management should be **systematic, science-based, and documented**
- The **level of effort and formality** should be **commensurate with risk**
- Decisions should be **transparent, traceable, and reviewable**
- Artificial intelligence does not alter these principles. What it alters is the **organization's ability to consistently apply them under real-world complexity**.

The most common audit failure related to QRM is not misuse of a tool—it is **inconsistent application of risk logic** across different decisions. AI, when properly governed, acts as a stabilizing force against this inconsistency.

19. AI and Risk Identification Under ICH Q9: Moving Beyond Obvious Risks

ICH Q9 expects organizations to identify risks that are **reasonably foreseeable**, not only those that have already resulted in failure. During audits, inspectors frequently probe whether risks were visible *before* an incident occurred.

20. The Human Limitation in Risk Identification

Human-led risk identification suffers from:

- Over-reliance on recent events
- Normalization of recurring "minor" issues
- Functional blind spots
- Organizational bias to avoid escalation
- As a result, many risks remain **latent** until an audit exposes them.

21. AI's Contribution: Weak Signal Detection

Artificial intelligence strengthens risk identification by detecting:

- Repeated minor deviations that share a common root
- Gradual drift in process parameters that remain within limits
- Documentation-execution mismatches across departments
- Training completion that does not correlate with performance
- These signals are individually insignificant but **collectively meaningful**. From an audit perspective, these are precisely the signals inspectors look for when they question the robustness of QRM.

Crucially, AI does not *define* a risk as critical—it **flags patterns** that require human evaluation. This preserves alignment with ICH Q9's emphasis on scientific judgment.

22. Risk Analysis: Where Most QRM Systems Collapse Under Audit Pressure

Risk analysis under ICH Q9 involves understanding the **likelihood and severity** of harm to product quality and patient safety. In practice, this often degenerates into mechanical scoring exercises.

23. Audit Observations Related to Weak Risk Analysis

Inspectors frequently identify:

- Identical risk scores applied to fundamentally different issues
- Risk ratings that do not reflect historical outcomes
- Inconsistent severity definitions across documents
- Down-grading of risks to avoid formal escalation
- These are not failures of methodology—they are failures of **risk discipline**.

24. How AI Supports Risk Analysis Without Violating Regulatory Expectations

AI enhances risk analysis by:

- Providing historical outcome data to contextualize probability
- Highlighting severity patterns based on actual impact
- Identifying discrepancies between assessed risk and realized consequences

- For example, if deviations classified as "low risk" consistently require extensive CAPAs, AI exposes this misalignment. The decision to reclassify the risk remains human—but the evidence becomes harder to ignore.

From an audit standpoint, this demonstrates **learning behavior**, which regulators view positively.

25. Risk Evaluation: Prioritization Under Scrutiny

Risk evaluation is where decisions become visible to inspectors. It is not enough to identify risks; organizations must show that they **prioritize correctly**.

26. Why Prioritization Fails During Audits

Common failure modes include:

- Treating all risks as equally urgent
- Prioritizing based on workload rather than impact
- Over-focusing on audit-visible risks
- Ignoring cumulative risk
- Inspectors are particularly sensitive to situations where:
- High-impact risks receive delayed attention
- Repeated issues are deprioritized due to familiarity

27. AI as a Risk Prioritization Consistency Tool

Artificial intelligence supports risk evaluation by:

- Aggregating risk indicators across systems
- Highlighting cumulative risk exposure

- Supporting proportional prioritization decisions
- Importantly, AI does not assign regulatory priority. It supports **consistency**, ensuring that similar risks are treated similarly over time.

This consistency is often what inspectors are really evaluating.

28. AI and Risk Control: Aligning Controls With Actual Risk

Risk control under ICH Q9 involves deciding whether risks should be:

- Reduced
- Accepted
- Avoided
- Transferred
- In pharmaceutical audits, inspectors frequently question whether controls are **justified, effective, and proportionate**.

29. Over-Control as an Audit Liability

Excessive controls often arise from:

- Fear-driven compliance
- Poor risk understanding
- Reactionary CAPAs
- Ironically, over-control can increase audit risk by:
- Obscuring accountability
- Creating procedural complexity
- Increasing opportunities for deviation

30. AI's Role in Control Effectiveness Assessment

AI supports risk control by:

- Identifying controls that fail to prevent recurrence
- Highlighting controls that add effort without risk reduction
- Supporting simplification aligned with actual risk
- This enables organizations to demonstrate **mature risk thinking**—a quality highly valued by inspectors.

31. Risk Review and Lifecycle Monitoring: The Audit Time Bomb

ICH Q9 clearly states that risk management is **not a one-time activity**. Risks must be reviewed as knowledge increases.

32.Audit Failures Linked to Static Risk Assessments

Inspectors often identify:

- Risk assessments that remain unchanged despite new data
- Failure to incorporate deviation trends
- No evidence of risk learning
- This is interpreted as **procedural compliance without system learning**.

33. AI as a Continuous Risk Review Mechanism

Artificial intelligence enables:

- Ongoing risk reassessment using live data
- Early detection of risk evolution
- Objective triggers for formal review

- This supports the concept of **living risk management**, directly aligned with ICH expectations.

34. Quality Risk Management During Live Audits: What Inspectors Actually Test

During audits, inspectors indirectly test QRM by asking questions such as:

- “How did you know this was a risk?”
- “Why was this considered low impact?”
- “What changed after the last deviation?”
- “How do you ensure this does not recur elsewhere?”
- Organizations supported by AI-enhanced QRM tend to respond with:
- Evidence-based explanations
- Consistent narratives
- Clear linkage between risk and control
- Those without it often rely on:
- Defensive explanations
- Isolated documents
- Personal reassurance
- Inspectors trust **systems**, not confidence.

35. AI and Data Integrity Risk Management During Audits

Data integrity is one of the most audit-sensitive risk domains. Failures here are rarely sudden—they are **progressive**.

36. Why Data Integrity Risks Evade Traditional QRM

Traditional QRM struggles with data integrity because:

- Risks manifest behaviorally
- Violations appear compliant on the surface
- Early indicators are subtle

37. AI as an Early Warning System for Data Integrity

AI supports data integrity risk management by:

- Detecting unusual data patterns
- Identifying inconsistent documentation behavior
- Highlighting systemic vulnerabilities
- This enables organizations to demonstrate **proactive control**, which regulators strongly favor.

38. Boundaries: What AI Must Never Do in QRM

To remain regulator-acceptable, AI must **never**:

- Override human judgment
- Auto-approve risk decisions
- Conceal negative signals
- Replace formal risk assessments
- AI must remain a **decision-support tool**, not a decision authority.

Failure to respect this boundary converts AI into a regulatory liability.

39. Cultural Impact: AI as a Risk Maturity Indicator

One of the most underestimated impacts of AI in QRM is cultural. AI systems tend to:

Reduce tolerance for weak reasoning

- Expose inconsistencies
- Encourage evidence-based discussion
- In organizations with mature quality culture, this is welcomed. In immature systems, it creates resistance.

Auditors can sense this difference.

40. Interim Conclusion: Risk Visibility Is the Real Regulatory Advantage

At this point, a central truth becomes clear:

Regulators do not penalize risk.
They penalize unmanaged, misunderstood, and ignored risk.

Artificial intelligence does not change regulatory expectations. It changes the organization's **ability to meet them consistently**.

41. Why Auditors Don't Fear Data—They Fear Blind Spots

Regulatory auditors are not alarmed by large volumes of data. They are alarmed by **gaps**, **inconsistencies**, and **unexplained patterns**.

From an audit perspective, the most common red flags are not catastrophic failures, but **signals of unmanaged risk**, such as:

- Deviations repeating across batches without escalation
- CAPAs closed on time but ineffective in reality

- Risk assessments that exist only at initiation, not during execution
- Trending performed quarterly, while risks evolve weekly
- Quality decisions based on experience instead of evidence

Traditional QRM systems often **record risk**, but fail to **observe it dynamically**.

This is where Artificial Intelligence changes the audit narrative—not by replacing Quality Risk Management, but by **making risk visible in real time**.

42. Static Risk Management vs Living Risk Management

43. Traditional QRM (Audit Reality)

In most pharmaceutical organizations:

- Risk assessments are created during:
- Change control initiation
    - Deviation opening
    - Technology transfer
    - Risk scores remain **unchanged** unless manually updated
- Controls are assumed effective until proven otherwise
- During audits, inspectors often ask:

"How do you know this risk remains under control today?"

This question exposes a structural weakness:

- Risk is treated as a **documented event**, not a **living condition**

44. AI-Enabled Living Risk Management

AI enables **continuous risk sensing** by:

- Observing process behavior over time
- Detecting weak signals before failure
- Correlating multiple quality events across systems
- Highlighting risk drift without human prompting
- In audit terms, this shifts QRM from:

  "We assessed the risk"
  to
  "We continuously observe the risk"

This distinction is subtle—and extremely powerful.

45. Risk Identification: From Human Memory to System Awareness

46. Audit Challenge

Auditors frequently challenge:

- Why certain risks were **not identified earlier**
- Why historical deviations did not inform future risk assessments
- Why similar issues keep recurring under different event IDs
- Human-led risk identification depends on:
- Experience
- Memory
- Availability of past records
- Cross-functional communication
- This creates blind spots.

47. AI's Role in Risk Identification

AI enhances risk identification by:

- Scanning historical deviations, complaints, OOS, CAPAs
- Detecting recurring patterns across products, processes, sites
- Identifying **latent risks** that never triggered formal deviation
- Examples of AI-supported risk signals:
- A process parameter drifting within limits but trending unfavorably
- Minor deviations clustering around specific operators or shifts
- CAPAs repeatedly addressing symptoms, not root causes
- Similar audit observations across multiple inspections
- During audits, this enables statements like:

"We identified this risk proactively based on system-wide trend analysis."

Which auditors recognize as **mature QRM behavior**.

48. Risk Analysis: Moving Beyond Subjective Scoring

49. The Problem with Traditional Risk Scoring

ICH Q9 allows qualitative and quantitative methods, but in practice:

- Severity, Occurrence, Detectability scores are often subjective
- Risk scoring varies by assessor
- Historical data is underutilized
- Auditors know this.

That's why they ask:

"How did you justify this risk score?"

50. How AI Strengthens Risk Analysis

AI does not redefine risk scoring—it **supports it with evidence**.

AI can:

- Use historical failure rates to inform occurrence scoring
- Analyze detection effectiveness based on past escapes
- Compare similar processes to normalize risk evaluation
- Flag inconsistencies in scoring logic across assessments
- Importantly:

Final risk acceptance remains human

- AI provides **context, not conclusions**
- In audits, this demonstrates:
- Decisions were data-informed
- Risk analysis was not arbitrary
- The organization understands its process behavior

51. Risk Control: Monitoring Effectiveness, Not Just Implementation

52. Audit Reality

Auditors do not ask:

"Did you implement a control?"

They ask:

"How do you know it works?"

Most CAPAs and controls fail audits because:

- Effectiveness checks are delayed
- Monitoring is manual and infrequent
- Metrics are disconnected from real risk

53. AI in Risk Control Monitoring

AI enables **control effectiveness surveillance** by:

- Continuously monitoring critical process indicators
- Detecting deviations from expected control behavior
- Linking CAPA actions to outcome trends
- Highlighting control fatigue or erosion
- This allows organizations to demonstrate:
- Controls are **actively monitored**
- Effectiveness is **verified over time**
- Failures are detected before escalation
- During audits, this supports a critical statement:

"We don't assume control effectiveness—we observe it."

54. Risk Communication: Speaking the Auditor's Language

55. Common Audit Failure

Organizations often struggle to:

- Explain complex risk landscapes clearly
- Connect risk assessments to operational reality
- Show how leadership is informed of evolving risks

- This leads to:
- Confusing explanations
- Overdocumentation
- Inconsistent messaging across departments

56. AI-Supported Risk Communication

AI improves risk communication by:

- Consolidating risk signals into coherent narratives
- Visualizing risk trends without overwhelming detail
- Aligning technical risk data with management understanding
- This supports:
- Management Review discussions
- Audit interviews
- Clear, consistent risk explanations
- Auditors value:
- Clarity over complexity
- Understanding over volume
- AI helps organizations **translate risk into insight.**

57. Risk Review: The Most Overlooked QRM Element

ICH Q9 emphasizes risk review, yet in practice:

- Reviews are periodic
- Triggered only by events
- Rarely proactive

- Auditors increasingly expect:
- Evidence that risks are revisited dynamically
- Adjustments based on emerging data
- Closure of outdated risk assumptions

58. AI as a Risk Review Trigger

AI supports risk review by:

- Alerting when assumptions no longer hold
- Detecting divergence between expected and actual outcomes
- Highlighting areas requiring reassessment
- This does not replace periodic reviews—it **activates them when needed**.

In audit terms:

- Risk review becomes responsive, not reactive
- Oversight becomes continuous, not ceremonial

59. What Auditors Actually See When AI Supports QRM

Auditors do not see algorithms.

They see outcomes:

- Fewer repeated observations
- Clearer risk rationales
- Better linkage between events
- Faster recognition of emerging issues
- More confident, consistent answers

They see:

- An organization **in control**
- A Quality System that **learns**
- Risk management that **evolves**

And most importantly:

- Professionals who understand their processes deeply

60. AI Does Not Reduce Accountability—It Increases It

A critical misconception is that AI reduces human responsibility.

In reality:

- AI increases visibility
- Visibility increases expectation
- Expectation increases accountability
- Auditors expect more from organizations that:
- Have access to better data
- Use advanced analytics
- Claim mature systems
- This is not a threat—it is a sign of trust.

61. Transitioning from Risk Documentation to Risk Stewardship

The ultimate shift enabled by AI is cultural.

From:

- Completing risk templates

  To:

- Stewarding process integrity
- From:
- Explaining failures
  To:
- Preventing them
- From:
- Audit survival
  To:
- Audit confidence
- Quality Risk Management becomes not a compliance task, but a **leadership responsibility**.

**PART 4
AI, Risk-Based Auditing & Changing Inspector Expectations**

62.The Silent Shift in How Audits Are Conducted

Regulatory audits are no longer purely checklist-driven. Across global agencies, inspections have quietly shifted toward **risk-based prioritization**.

Inspectors today:

- Spend less time verifying existence of procedures
- Spend more time assessing **system behavior**
- Follow **risk signals**, not documents
- This means:
- Areas with historical issues get deeper scrutiny
- Trends matter more than isolated events
- Data coherence matters more than volume

- Artificial Intelligence aligns naturally with this shift—not because inspectors demand AI, but because **AI supports the same risk-focused thinking inspectors already use**.

63. How Inspectors Prioritize Risk During Audits

Inspectors typically focus on:

- Repeating deviations or observations
- Ineffective CAPAs
- Poor trend detection
- Weak management oversight
- Disconnect between documented risk and operational reality
- AI-supported QRM systems help organizations:
- Identify these risk zones internally
- Address them before inspections
- Present a coherent control narrative
- Auditors do not ask:

"Do you use AI?"

They ask:

"How do you know where your biggest risks are?"

AI simply helps answer that question honestly.

64. Risk-Based Sampling and AI Readiness

Modern inspections rely heavily on:

- Sampling
- Traceability

- Cross-referencing systems
- When AI supports QRM:
- Risk-high processes are already flagged internally
- Sampling logic aligns with internal assessments
- Inspectors encounter **fewer surprises**
- This alignment reduces:
- Defensive explanations
- On-the-spot justifications
- Perceived loss of control
- The audit becomes a **confirmation exercise**, not a discovery mission.

65. Inspector Confidence vs Organizational Confidence

Auditors gain confidence when they see:

- Consistent answers across teams
- Clear awareness of vulnerabilities
- Evidence of proactive oversight
- AI indirectly strengthens this by:
- Reducing reliance on individual memory
- Creating shared visibility
- Supporting consistent decision-making
- Confidence is contagious in audits.
  AI helps organizations project it—authentically.

****PART 5**
Common AI–QRM Pitfalls That Trigger 483s**

66. Over-Automation Without Governance

One of the fastest ways to lose auditor trust is:

- Automating risk decisions without clear ownership
- Auditors expect:
- Humans to remain accountable
- Decisions to be explainable
- Overrides to be justified
- AI must support, not replace, GMP judgment.

67. Black-Box Risk Decisions

If quality teams cannot explain:

- Why a risk was flagged
- Why a trend was escalated
- Why a signal was ignored
- Then the system becomes a liability.

Transparency matters more than sophistication.

68. Using AI Without Updating SOPs

A frequent audit gap:

- Advanced analytics operating outside procedural control
- Auditors expect:
- SOPs to reflect actual practices
- Clear definition of AI's role in QRM
- Documented review and approval mechanisms
- Uncontrolled innovation equals uncontrolled risk.

69. Treating AI Outputs as "Truth"

AI outputs are indicators—not conclusions.

When organizations:

- Accept AI signals without challenge
- Fail to contextualize outputs
- Ignore process knowledge
- They weaken their own QRM credibility.

Auditors value **critical thinking**, not blind acceptance.

70. Fragmented AI Usage Across Departments

Disconnected AI initiatives create:

- Inconsistent risk signals
- Conflicting narratives
- Audit confusion
- QRM must remain **integrated**, not departmentalized.

****PART 6**
Building an Audit-Defensible AI-Enabled QRM Framework**

71. Start with QRM Principles—Not Technology

The foundation must always be:

- ICH Q9 principles
- Risk proportionality
- Scientific understanding
- Lifecycle thinking
- AI should be mapped **onto** QRM—never the reverse.

72. Clear Role Definition

An audit-ready AI-QRM framework clearly defines:

- What AI can observe
- What humans decide
- Who approves outcomes
- How disagreements are resolved
- This clarity protects both compliance and careers.

73. Data Integrity as a Prerequisite

AI cannot compensate for:

- Poor data quality
- Incomplete records
- Inconsistent classifications
- Inspectors will trace AI insights back to raw data. Data integrity remains non-negotiable.

74. Governance and Oversight

Audit-defensible frameworks include:

- Periodic review of AI performance
- Change control for AI logic
- Validation proportional to risk
- Management oversight
- Governance builds trust—internally and externally.

75. Training the Human System

AI readiness is not a software issue—it is a **people issue.**

Quality professionals must understand:

- What AI does
- What it does not do
- How to interpret outputs
- When to challenge results
- Auditors observe competence more than tools.

**PART 7
Career Impact: How AI-Enabled QRM Protects Professionals**

76. Audits Are Personal—Whether We Admit It or Not

483s and Warning Letters do not just impact companies. They impact:

- Reputations
- Career trajectories
- Professional confidence
- AI-supported QRM reduces:
- Last-minute firefighting
- Defensive explanations
- Individual blame
- It distributes awareness—and responsibility.

77. From Firefighter to Risk Leader

Professionals using AI-supported QRM:

- Spend less time reacting
- Spend more time anticipating

- Speak with evidence, not assumptions
- Auditors recognize maturity.
  So do organizations.

78. Accountability Without Anxiety

AI does not remove accountability.

It removes uncertainty.

And uncertainty is what creates audit anxiety.

**PART 8
The Mature End State: Calm Audits, Confident Systems**

In a mature AI-enabled QRM environment:

- Risks are visible early
- Controls are monitored continuously
- Decisions are explainable
- Audits are predictable

Not because systems are perfect—but because they are **understood**.

79. Final Reflection for Chapter 19

Quality Risk Management is not about avoiding risk.

It is about **owning it responsibly**.

Artificial Intelligence does not change the principles of QRM.

It strengthens their execution.

In the eyes of regulators, the strongest systems are not the most automated—they are the most **aware**.

Chapter 20

Artificial Intelligence and CAPA Remediation During Pharmaceutical Audits

1. CAPA: The True Measure of a Quality System

In pharmaceutical audits, deviations are expected.

Errors occur. Systems fail. Processes drift.

What regulators truly evaluate is not the **absence of problems**, but the **quality of response**.

Corrective and Preventive Action (CAPA) systems are therefore not peripheral quality tools. They are the **central nervous system** of a Pharmaceutical Quality System.

Auditors repeatedly state—explicitly and implicitly—that:

- Weak CAPA systems lead to repeat observations
- Repeat observations lead to Warning Letters
- Warning Letters signal loss of control
- Artificial Intelligence does not redefine CAPA requirements. It reshapes how organizations **understand, execute, and sustain remediation**—especially under audit scrutiny.

2. Why CAPA Fails in Otherwise "Compliant" Organizations

Many organizations with certified systems, validated processes, and experienced staff still struggle with CAPA effectiveness.

Audits frequently reveal:

- CAPAs closed on time but ineffective
- Root causes that address symptoms, not systems
- Preventive actions that do not prevent recurrence
- Trend-based CAPAs triggered too late
- Ownership confusion across functions
- These failures are rarely due to lack of intent. They arise from **structural limitations of human-driven systems**.

CAPA failure is not a people problem.
It is a **visibility and connectivity problem**.

3. CAPA in the Auditor's Mindset

Auditors do not evaluate CAPA as a checklist activity.

They evaluate:

- Whether the organization *learns*
- Whether it *remembers*
- Whether it *changes behavior*
- Typical audit questions include:
- "How did you determine this was the root cause?"
- "How do you know this CAPA is effective?"
- "Why did this issue recur after closure?"

- "What similar risks were assessed elsewhere?"
- CAPA is therefore the **lens through which auditors judge maturity**.

4. The Structural Weakness of Traditional CAPA Systems

Traditional CAPA systems suffer from predictable limitations:

a) Linear Thinking in Non-Linear Systems

Quality events are interconnected.
CAPAs are often treated as isolated responses.

b) Root Cause Bias

Investigations depend heavily on:

- Investigator experience
- Time pressure
- Organizational culture
- This introduces unconscious bias.

c) Fragmented Data Sources

Deviation records, complaints, audit findings, process data, and change controls often exist in silos.

Human investigators cannot realistically correlate all of them.

d) Delayed Learning

CAPA effectiveness is often assessed months later—sometimes after recurrence.

5. Where Artificial Intelligence Fits—and Where It Does Not

Artificial Intelligence **does not**:

- Decide root cause
- Approve CAPAs
- Replace investigation teams
- Override GMP judgment
- Artificial Intelligence **does**:
- Enhance signal detection
- Improve pattern recognition
- Support evidence-based reasoning
- Monitor effectiveness continuously
- In audits, this distinction matters deeply.

6. AI and CAPA Triggering: Detecting Issues Earlier

CAPA initiation is often reactive.

AI supports **earlier triggering** by:

- Detecting deviation clusters
- Identifying complaint patterns
- Highlighting repeat minor issues
- Observing process drift before failure
- This enables:
- Preventive CAPAs instead of corrective-only actions
- Trend-based interventions
- Reduced severity escalation

- Auditors view early CAPA initiation as a sign of **control**, not weakness.

7. AI-Supported Root Cause Analysis (RCA)

Root cause analysis is the most scrutinized CAPA element.

7.1 The Human Challenge in RCA

Investigators often face:

- Limited time
- Pressure to close
- Incomplete data visibility
- Cognitive bias toward familiar causes

7.2 How AI Supports RCA

AI assists by:

- Analyzing historical CAPAs for similar patterns
- Correlating process parameters with deviations
- Identifying systemic contributors
- Highlighting overlooked data relationships
- AI does not say *"this is the root cause."*
  It says *"these patterns are statistically relevant."*

The decision remains human.

8. CAPA Design: From Action Lists to System Corrections

Auditors increasingly criticize CAPAs that:

- Retrain operators repeatedly
- Revise SOPs without behavior change

- Add checks instead of removing root causes
- AI helps distinguish:
- Local fixes vs systemic solutions
- High-impact actions vs cosmetic actions
- Sustainable controls vs temporary barriers
- This leads to **stronger CAPA design**, which auditors recognize quickly.

9. Preventive Action: The Most Misunderstood CAPA Element

Preventive action is often misunderstood as:

- A future correction
- A risk assessment formality
- A documentation exercise
- AI enables **true prevention** by:
- Identifying risk propagation paths
- Highlighting vulnerable processes
- Learning from near-misses
- Anticipating failure modes
- This aligns directly with ICH Q9 and Q10 expectations.

10. CAPA Effectiveness: The Audit's Deciding Factor

Auditors may accept:

- Imperfect investigations
- Conservative timelines

- Complex issues
- They rarely accept **ineffective CAPAs**.

10.1 Traditional Effectiveness Checks

Often limited to:

- Single-time verification
- Short observation windows
- Subjective confirmation

10.2 AI-Enabled Effectiveness Monitoring

AI enables:

- Continuous monitoring of relevant indicators
- Early detection of recurrence
- Measurement of control sustainability
- Comparison against baseline behavior
- Auditors trust systems that **observe outcomes**, not just actions.

11. CAPA During Live Audits: What Changes with AI

During inspections, AI-supported CAPA systems allow teams to:

- Explain decisions confidently
- Demonstrate historical learning
- Show cross-system awareness
- Respond calmly to deep questioning
- Auditors notice:
- Reduced defensiveness
- Clear ownership

- Evidence-based reasoning
- AI does not impress auditors.
  Control does.

12. CAPA Traceability and Knowledge Retention

One of the biggest CAPA failures is **organizational amnesia**.

AI improves retention by:

- Linking CAPAs across time
- Preventing duplicate investigations
- Preserving rationale
- Enabling future reference
- Auditors often ask:

"How did you ensure this lesson was applied elsewhere?"

AI-supported systems answer that question convincingly.

13. AI, CAPA, and Management Review

CAPA effectiveness is ultimately a **management responsibility**.

AI strengthens management oversight by:

- Aggregating CAPA health metrics
- Highlighting systemic weaknesses
- Enabling risk-based prioritization
- Supporting informed decisions
- This aligns directly with ICH Q10 expectations.

14. Data Integrity and AI-Supported CAPA

AI depends on data integrity—but also reinforces it.

- Poor data quality becomes visible faster.
  Inconsistencies surface sooner.
- Auditors view this transparency as maturity, not failure—**if managed properly**.

15. Validation and Governance Expectations

AI supporting CAPA must operate within:

- Defined SOPs
- Controlled change management
- Appropriate validation
- Clear accountability
- Auditors expect:
- Proportional validation
- Explainability
- Oversight, not autonomy
- Governance protects credibility.

16. Common AI–CAPA Mistakes That Trigger Observations

- Treating AI outputs as conclusions
- Automating decisions without review
- Failing to update procedures
- Over-reliance on metrics
- Lack of investigator understanding

- These failures are avoidable.

17. Career Impact: CAPA as a Professional Risk Zone

CAPA failures are personal.

- Names appear in reports.
  Decisions are remembered.
- AI-supported CAPA systems:
- Reduce individual exposure
- Distribute knowledge
- Support defensible decisions
- Enable professional confidence
- This matters more than technology.

18. From CAPA Closure to CAPA Learning

The most mature organizations treat CAPA not as:

- A closure requirement
- But as:
- A learning mechanism
- A system-improvement engine
- A trust-building process
- AI accelerates learning—but humans must act.

19. The Regulator's Unspoken Expectation

Regulators do not expect perfection.
They expect:

- Awareness

- Responsibility
- Consistency
- Learning
- AI helps organizations meet these expectations—quietly.

20. Final Reflection: CAPA Is Where Trust Is Earned

CAPA systems reveal:

- How organizations think
- How they respond to pressure
- How they protect patients
- Artificial Intelligence does not replace CAPA ownership. It strengthens it.

In audits, the strongest organizations are not those with fewer deviations—but those that **never repeat the same mistake twice**.

Conclusion

From Audit Survival to Quality Stewardship

Pharmaceutical audits have never been merely technical exercises.

They have always been reflections of organizational behavior.

Behind every observation lies a decision.

Behind every decision lies a system.

Behind every system lies a mindset.

This book was not written to teach artificial intelligence.

It was written to examine **how quality systems behave under pressure**, and how modern organizations can regain **control, clarity, and confidence** in an increasingly complex regulatory environment.

Artificial Intelligence appears throughout this book not as a hero, nor as a disruptor, but as a **mirror**—reflecting patterns that already exist, revealing risks that already matter, and exposing gaps that were always there.

The Audit Was Never the Real Problem

For decades, professionals have framed audits as adversarial events:

- Inspectors versus organizations
- Findings versus explanations
- Compliance versus operations
- This framing has done quiet damage.

It has trained quality teams to:

- Prepare for audits instead of preparing systems
- Focus on answers instead of understanding

- React instead of observe
- Defend instead of learn
- Audits became stressful not because regulators changed— but because **systems stopped being transparent to their own owners**.

The fear surrounding audits is rarely about inspectors.

It is about **uncertainty**.

Uncertainty about:

- What inspectors might find
- Whether controls actually work
- Whether explanations will hold
- Whether past decisions will be questioned
- This uncertainty is the true enemy of audit confidence.

Why Traditional Quality Systems Struggle Today

Pharmaceutical Quality Systems were designed in a different era.

An era where:

- Data volumes were manageable
- Processes changed slowly
- Human memory could compensate for system gaps
- Paper trails evolved linearly
- Today's environment is fundamentally different:
- Data is continuous and multi-dimensional
- Processes are interconnected across sites and suppliers
- Decisions accumulate faster than they can be reviewed

- Risks evolve silently, not suddenly
- Yet many organizations still rely on:
- Periodic reviews to manage continuous risk
- Static risk assessments to explain dynamic behavior
- Human recall to connect systemic issues
- Closure-based metrics to judge effectiveness
- These approaches are not wrong.
  They are simply **no longer sufficient on their own**.

Artificial Intelligence as a Structural Response, Not a Trend

Artificial Intelligence entered pharmaceutical quality not because it was fashionable, but because **human-only oversight reached its natural limits**.

AI did not create complexity.
Complexity already existed.

AI did not introduce risk.
Risk was already present.

AI simply made both **visible**.

This is why mature regulators do not fear AI.
They fear **unobserved systems**.

AI, when governed properly, does something profoundly important:

- It reduces dependency on individual vigilance
- It converts fragmented signals into coherent patterns
- It reveals weak trends before they become failures
- It transforms hindsight into foresight

- Not by replacing judgment—
  but by **supporting it continuously**.

The Central Theme: Visibility Before Control

Across all chapters—whether discussing audits, QRM, CAPA, data integrity, or management review—one principle emerges consistently:

You cannot control what you cannot see.

Traditional systems often give the illusion of control through:

- Documentation
- Procedures
- Certifications
- Completion metrics
- But audits rarely fail due to missing documents.
  They fail due to **misalignment between documents and reality**.

AI-supported systems reduce this gap by:

- Observing behavior, not just recording intent
- Monitoring effectiveness, not just implementation
- Connecting events across time and departments
- Making risk evolution visible
- This visibility changes everything.

Risk Management Revisited: From Forms to Awareness

Quality Risk Management was never meant to be a paperwork exercise. ICH Q9 never intended risk to be frozen at initiation.

Yet over time, QRM drifted into:

- One-time assessments
- Subjective scoring
- Event-triggered reviews
- Procedural compliance
- Artificial Intelligence reclaims the original intent of QRM:
- Continuous awareness
- Data-informed judgment
- Dynamic reassessment
- Proportional response
- This is not a technological upgrade.
  It is a **conceptual correction**.

Auditors recognize this immediately—not because of algorithms, but because **risk narratives become coherent**.

CAPA: Where Systems Reveal Their True Maturity

If risk management reflects awareness,
CAPA reflects **learning**.

CAPA systems fail not because organizations do not act—
but because actions do not always change outcomes.

The recurring audit question:

> "Why did this happen again?"

is not an accusation.
It is an invitation to examine whether learning truly occurred.

AI strengthens CAPA by:

- Exposing systemic contributors

- Challenging superficial root causes
- Monitoring effectiveness beyond closure
- Preserving organizational memory
- This transforms CAPA from:
- A remediation obligation
  into
- A system-improvement mechanism
- Auditors trust organizations that **remember**.

Data Integrity: The Silent Backbone

Throughout the book, one truth remains constant:

Artificial Intelligence cannot compensate for poor data integrity.
But it can expose it faster.

This exposure is not a weakness.
It is a safeguard.

Organizations that embrace AI-supported oversight accept an uncomfortable truth:

- Weak data will surface
- Inconsistencies will become visible
- Assumptions will be challenged
- This is not risk amplification—it is **risk recognition**.

Regulators do not penalize transparency.
They penalize **uncontrolled opacity**.

Governance: The Line Between Support and Liability

Technology without governance creates vulnerability.

This book deliberately avoided positioning AI as autonomous or decision-making.
Because in regulated environments, autonomy without accountability is not innovation—it is negligence.

Audit-defensible AI systems are characterized by:

- Clear human ownership
- Explainable logic
- Proportional validation
- Change control
- Management oversight
- AI becomes credible not when it is powerful,
  but when it is **controlled**.

The Human Role Has Never Been More Important

One of the most dangerous misconceptions is that AI diminishes the role of quality professionals.

In reality, it **raises expectations**.

With better visibility comes:

- Higher accountability
- Stronger scrutiny
- Less tolerance for ignorance
- Greater emphasis on judgment

- AI does not make quality professionals replaceable.
  It makes **passive oversight impossible**.

The future belongs to professionals who:

- Understand their systems deeply
- Interpret data critically
- Challenge outputs responsibly
- Lead quality conversations confidently
- Auditors do not audit software.
  They audit **people operating systems**.

Career Impact: The Unspoken Reality

Quality failures are rarely abstract.
They are personal.

Names appear in reports.
Decisions are questioned years later.
Careers are shaped by audit outcomes.

This book addressed AI not only as a compliance tool, but as a **professional safeguard**.

By:

- Reducing individual blind spots
- Distributing system awareness
- Supporting defensible decisions
- Encouraging proactive action
- AI does not remove responsibility—
  it reduces **unnecessary exposure to uncertainty**.

From Audit Survival to Audit Confidence

Audit survival is reactive.

It is characterized by:

- Last-minute preparation
- Data scrambling
- Defensive explanations
- Emotional exhaustion
- Audit confidence is proactive.

It emerges when:

- Systems are understood
- Risks are visible
- CAPAs are effective
- Decisions are traceable
- Leadership is informed
- Artificial Intelligence supports this transition quietly—not by guaranteeing success, but by **reducing unpredictability**.

Predictable systems produce predictable audits.

The Regulator's Perspective, Reconsidered

Regulators are not seeking:

- Perfect systems
- Zero deviations
- Advanced technology
- They are seeking:
- Control

- Awareness
- Responsibility
- Learning
- Organizations that use AI responsibly signal maturity because they acknowledge a fundamental truth:

Human oversight alone is no longer sufficient for modern complexity.

This acknowledgment is not weakness.
It is **professional honesty**.

The Ethical Dimension

At its core, pharmaceutical quality is not about audits.
It is about patients.

Every undetected trend,
every ineffective CAPA,
every ignored signal

carries potential consequences beyond compliance.

AI, when used ethically, strengthens:

- Patient protection
- Product consistency
- System resilience
- Organizational accountability
- Technology does not create ethics—but it can support ethical behavior by **removing ignorance as an excuse**.

A Quiet but Profound Shift

This book does not argue that every organization must adopt advanced AI tomorrow.

It argues something more fundamental:

That the future of pharmaceutical quality lies in:

- Continuous awareness
- System thinking
- Evidence-based decisions
- Calm accountability
- Artificial Intelligence is one path to that future—not the destination itself.

Final Reflection

Audits will continue.
Regulations will evolve.
Technology will advance.

But one principle will remain unchanged:

> Quality systems must understand themselves.

Organizations that achieve this understanding do not fear audits. They welcome them as confirmations.

Artificial Intelligence, used wisely, does not make systems complex. It makes complexity **manageable**.

And in regulated environments,
manageability is the foundation of trust.

Bibliography

International Council for Harmonisation of Technical Requirements for Pharmaceuticals for Human Use (ICH). *ICH Q8(R2): Pharmaceutical Development.* ICH Harmonised Guideline. Available at: https://database.ich.org/sites/default/files/Q8_R2_Guideline.pdf

International Council for Harmonisation of Technical Requirements for Pharmaceuticals for Human Use (ICH). *ICH Q9(R1): Quality Risk Management.* ICH Harmonised Guideline, Step 4, 2020. Available at: https://database.ich.org/sites/default/files/ICH_Q9-R1_Guideline_Step4_2020_1116.pdf

International Council for Harmonisation of Technical Requirements for Pharmaceuticals for Human Use (ICH). *ICH Q10: Pharmaceutical Quality System.* ICH Harmonised Guideline. Available at: https://database.ich.org/sites/default/files/Q10_Guideline.pdf

International Council for Harmonisation of Technical Requirements for Pharmaceuticals for Human Use (ICH). *ICH Q11: Development and Manufacture of Drug Substances.* ICH Harmonised Guideline. Available at: https://database.ich.org/sites/default/files/Q11_Guideline.pdf

International Council for Harmonisation of Technical Requirements for Pharmaceuticals for Human Use (ICH). *ICH Q12: Technical and Regulatory Considerations for*

Pharmaceutical Product Lifecycle Management.
ICH Harmonised Guideline.
Available at: https://database.ich.org/sites/default/files/Q12_Guideline.pdf

International Council for Harmonisation of Technical Requirements for Pharmaceuticals for Human Use (ICH).
ICH M4Q(R1): Common Technical Document for the Registration of Pharmaceuticals for Human Use – Quality.
ICH Harmonised Guideline.
Available at: https://database.ich.org/sites/default/files/M4Q_R1_Guideline.pdf

International Council for Harmonisation of Technical Requirements for Pharmaceuticals for Human Use (ICH).
ICH M7(R2): Assessment and Control of DNA Reactive (Mutagenic) Impurities.
ICH Harmonised Guideline.
Available at: https://database.ich.org/sites/default/files/ICH_M7_R2_Guideline.pdf

International Council for Harmonisation of Technical Requirements for Pharmaceuticals for Human Use (ICH).
ICH M15: Model-Informed Drug Development.
ICH Harmonised Guideline, Step 4, 2024.
Available at: https://database.ich.org/sites/default/files/ICH_M15_Guideline_Step4_2024.pdf

Regulatory & Inspection Authorities

U.S. Food and Drug Administration (FDA).
Quality Systems Approach to Pharmaceutical CGMP Regulations.
Available at: https://www.fda.gov/media/71023/download

U.S. Food and Drug Administration (FDA).
Data Integrity and Compliance With Drug CGMP.
Guidance for Industry.
Available at: https://www.fda.gov/media/119267/download

U.S. Food and Drug Administration (FDA).
Artificial Intelligence and Machine Learning in Drug Development.
Discussion Paper.
Available at: https://www.fda.gov/media/145022/download

European Medicines Agency (EMA).
Guideline on Computerised Systems and Electronic Data in Clinical Trials.
Available at: https://www.ema.europa.eu/en/documents/scientific-guideline/guideline-computerised-systems-electronic-data-clinical-trials_en.pdf

European Medicines Agency (EMA).
Reflection Paper on the Use of Artificial Intelligence in the Medicinal Product Lifecycle.
Available at: https://www.ema.europa.eu/en/documents/regulatory-procedural-guideline/reflection-paper-use-artificial-intelligence-medicinal-product-lifecycle_en.pdf

Pharmaceutical Inspection Co-operation Scheme (PIC/S).
PI 011: Good Practices for Computerised Systems in Regulated GxP Environments.
Available at: https://picscheme.org/docview/344

International Standards & Quality Systems

International Organization for Standardization (ISO).
ISO 9001: Quality Management Systems—Requirements.
Available at: https://www.iso.org/standard/62085.html

International Organization for Standardization (ISO).
ISO 31000: Risk Management—Guidelines.
Available at: https://www.iso.org/standard/65694.html

International Organization for Standardization (ISO).
ISO/IEC 27001: Information Security Management Systems.
Available at: https://www.iso.org/standard/54534.html

World Health Organization (WHO)

World Health Organization (WHO).
WHO Technical Report Series No. 996: Annex 5 – Quality Risk Management.
Available at: https://www.who.int/publications/i/item/WHO-TRS-996

World Health Organization (WHO).
Guidelines on Data Integrity.
Available at: https://www.who.int/publications/i/item/WHO-MVP-EMP-2016.02

Artificial Intelligence & Governance

Organisation for Economic Co-operation and Development (OECD).
OECD Principles on Artificial Intelligence.
Available at: https://oecd.ai/en/ai-principles

European Commission.
Ethics Guidelines for Trustworthy Artificial Intelligence.
Available at: https://digital-strategy.ec.europa.eu/en/library/ethics-guidelines-trustworthy-ai

www.ingramcontent.com/pod-product-compliance
Ingram Content Group UK Ltd.
Pitfield, Milton Keynes, MK11 3LW, UK
UKHW020421061026
15625UKWH00006B/345

9 798904 316563